4X Your E-Commerce SALES IN 169 DAYS

4X Your E-Commerce SALES IN 169 DAYS

CA Rajev Harlalka

Available on amazonkindle

Worldwide Published by

Pendown Press
PREMIUM BUSINESS PUBLISHER

PENDOWN PRESS LLP

An ISO 9001 & ISO 14001 Certified Co.,
Regd. Office: 3767A, Kanhaiya Nagar,
Tri Nagar, Delhi-110035
Ph.: 8130886000, 9650072927
E-mail: info@pendownpress.com
Branch Office: 1A/2A, 20, Hari Sadan, Ansari Road,
Daryaganj, New Delhi-110002
Ph.: 011-45794768
Website: PendownPress.com

Edition: 2025
Price: ₹ 496
ISBN: 978-93-6338-036-3

Layout and Cover Designed by Pendown Graphics Team
Printed and Bound in India by Thomson Press India Ltd.

For the ones who believe in the power of e-commerce, may this book be your roadmap to success. May your passion turn into profit, and your ideas into reality. Keep innovating, keep disrupting, and keep pushing the boundaries of what's possible.

CONTENTS

Introduction

Welcome, dear reader, to the journey that lies ahead.

I am **Rajev Harlalka**, a practicing Chartered Accountant with a robust professional experience of 20 years, I've delved deep into the realm of entrepreneurship and business management, gaining firsthand experience of the unique challenges and opportunities that come with them.

Entrepreneurs are often drawn to new business prospects without fully appreciating the complexities of the industry. It is like setting sail in uncharted waters without a compass. While their spirit of exploration is commendable, understanding the intricacies of the business environment can make the difference between smooth sailing and stormy seas. This is where the role of a seasoned professional, like a Chartered Accountant, becomes instrumental.

Over the years, the focus has been on helping business owners navigate the complex world of accounting, taxation, and compliance, providing the tools and guidance needed to build stronger, more resilient enterprises. This journey of nurturing and aiding businesses has been both challenging and rewarding.

The rise of e-commerce has drastically transformed the business landscape. In the role of an Amazon RCA (Recommended Chartered Accountant), there has been an opportunity to work with a wide spectrum of e-commerce sellers across platforms like Amazon, Flipkart, Myntra, Meesho, Ajio, JIO Mart, and more, from fledgling startups to established brands. This experience has given me a rich perspective into their world, revealing the unique challenges and the immense potential that the e-commerce industry holds.

In contrast to traditional business models, e-commerce presents a distinct set of challenges and opportunities. Sellers need to register themselves in multiple states to penetrate deeper into the market and reach a wider customer base. While this strategy can drive business growth, it also brings along a host of taxation and compliance responsibilities.

In this complex, ever-evolving landscape, what an e-commerce entrepreneur truly needs is a trusted companion - someone who can provide not just expertise and guidance, but also care and support in all circumstances.

This book, “4X Your E-Commerce Sales in 169 Days,” aims to be your reliable guide through the world of e-commerce. It’s packed with practical advice to help you tackle compliance and taxation challenges, boost your sales, and draw inspiration from successful e-commerce stories.

Acknowledgements

First and foremost, I want to extend my deepest gratitude to my father, Mr. R.K. Harlalka. His exceptional wisdom and unending patience planted the seed of curiosity in me and laid the foundation upon which I have built my dreams. His values, resilience, and vision for success have been a guiding light throughout my journey. Thank you, Papaji, for being my rock.

To my wonderful wife, Payal, you have been my anchor amidst the storm, providing constant support, understanding, and love that have made all the difference. Your unwavering faith in my abilities, your sacrifices, and your silent prayers have been the pillars that upheld me during the process of bringing this book to life. Thank you for being my safe harbor.

To my adorable children, Harsh and Khushi, you are the joy of my life and the fuel to my aspirations. Your innocent questions, contagious laughter, and refreshing perspective on life keep me grounded and remind me every day of what truly matters. Your sparkling eyes inspire me to dream bigger and work harder. Thank you for being my inspiration.

I'm deeply grateful to my coach, Mr. Akshar Yadav, whose guidance has been nothing short of extraordinary. His expertise, constant encouragement, and sharp insights have been pivotal in shaping this book and my journey. His unwavering belief in my potential has pushed me beyond my limits. Thank you, Akshar, for helping me elevate my vision and my purpose.

To my mentoring group members, your relentless pursuit of excellence and your constructive feedback have played a significant role in completing this book on time. The dynamic discussions, collaborative brainstorming sessions, and mutual learning have been instrumental in fine-tuning my thoughts and ideas. Thank you for motivating me, pushing me, challenging me, and walking with me on this path.

Lastly, to my GIL Achievers Table members, I owe a debt of gratitude for your persistent motivation and for reminding me to always aim high. Your success stories, your perseverance, and your spirit of camaraderie have been a constant source of motivation. Thank you for being my cheerleaders and my critics, for helping me maintain my focus and for always challenging me to do better.

Each of you, in your unique way, has contributed to this endeavor, and for that, I am eternally grateful. I am a better person, writer, and dreamer because of you. Thank you!.

With Love & Admiration,

CA Rajev Harlalka

You don't need forever to
change your business.
You need 169 days of
absolute obsession.

CHAPTER 1

WHY THIS BOOK

In today's busy digital marketplace, it is essential to have a clear and effective strategy to drive e-commerce sales. That's why we have put together *"4X Your E-commerce Sales in 169 Days*" - a guide designed to help you navigate the complex online business landscape and rapidly grow your business in less than six months.

In the last decade, the e-commerce sector has witnessed remarkable growth, driven by advancements in technology, changing consumer behaviors, and the global pandemic's impact. The ability to purchase items from the comfort of your home has transformed the way businesses operate, and customers shop. However, while these changes have given businesses new opportunities to reach a global market, they have also made the online market really tough.

In this competitive market, businesses must adapt to survive, and more importantly, to thrive. To succeed, you must understand not only the basics of e-commerce but also how to leverage digital marketing, customer acquisition, and retention strategies. It is not just about being online; it's about being easy to find, being engaging, and turning people who just look around into buyers, and people who buy into loyal customers.

The purpose of this book is simple: to equip you with a comprehensive, step-by-step guide that can help you increase your e-commerce sales by four times within a specific timeframe of 169 days. Why 169 days? This timeline presents not only a challenge but also a realistic opportunity for significant growth when the right strategies and tools are applied consistently and with determination.

This book isn't about easy solutions or shortcuts to success. Instead, it offers a deep dive into understanding the mechanisms of the e-commerce world. It's about building a strong foundation and implementing systematic, strategic, and customer-centered tactics to boost your sales, increase profit margins, and nurture customer loyalty. It's your roadmap to crafting your own success story within the vast landscape of e-commerce.

In the upcoming chapters, you'll find out about the important things you need to know to make your e-commerce business successful. From promoting your products using digital marketing to customer acquisition and retention, and making more sales from those customers. This book is designed as a kind of roadmap, filled with actionable strategies, practical advice, and real-world case studies to inspire you and guide you on your journey to e-commerce success.

So, let's embark on this journey together, as we unfold the secrets and strategies to 4X Your E-commerce Sales in 169 Days.

The Promise of E-commerce

E-commerce is not just another trend that emerged in the digital age; it is a game changer that has completely changed how businesses operate and how customers interact with those businesses. E-commerce brings the promise of boundless opportunities, with a global market that keeps growing and is easy to access.

E-commerce's magic is in how it erases the geographical boundaries and keeps running 24/7, offering unparalleled convenience to the customers. It's not just for big players—small businesses can also thrive and startups can shine by blending creativity and online marketing smarts.

E-commerce also promises the ability to personalize the customer experience at a larger scale. With data analytics, businesses can learn about their customers' behaviors and preferences, allowing them to adjust their marketing strategies and product offerings to meet individual customer needs.

However, the true potential of e-commerce goes beyond these operational benefits. It sets the stage where constant innovation is rewarded. With the right tactics, each point of interaction on your e-commerce platform presents an opportunity to surpass customer expectations, build their trust, and foster their loyalty.

Also, thanks to the rise of social media and digital advertising platforms, promoting your e-commerce business has become easier than it used to be.

Brands can engage with their customers in real-time, resolve issues, gather feedback, and create a community around their products and services.

In spite of these promises, e-commerce is not without its challenges. The digital marketplace is full of competition, with countless businesses competing for the attention of consumers. This is where a book like "4X Your E-commerce Sales in 169 Days" proves its worth. This book will guide you in understanding the potential of e-commerce and overcoming its challenges.

The promise of e-commerce is not just about maintaining an online presence; it's about utilizing the power of digital platforms to drive growth and profitability.

By following the strategies and guidelines in this book, you will be able to unlock this potential and maximize the promise of e-commerce for your business. Thus, we begin our journey towards quadrupling your e-commerce sales in just 169 days.

Why 169 Days?

As you begin your journey to quadruple your e-commerce sales, you might wonder, why specifically 169 days? The answer is two-fold. Firstly, 169 days represents a clear and measurable timeline, providing a sense of urgency and focus. Secondly, this period, roughly equivalent to half a year, allows ample time for strategic planning, implementation, and assessment of the results.

In the world of business, setting specific, measurable, achievable, relevant, and time-bound (SMART) goals is crucial to success. The timeline of 169 days meets these criteria - it's specific, measurable, achievable, relevant and time-bound. It gives you a clear timeframe to work towards, rather than leaving your success to an uncertain future.

One might argue that business growth should be viewed from a long-term perspective, and rightly so. However, setting a mid-term goal like this can act as a stepping stone towards that long-term success. The 169-day timeline is a challenge, pushing you to implement, monitor, and modify strategies more quickly, encouraging proactive decision-making and fostering a culture of agility and resilience within your organization.

Moreover, this period is long enough to allow for meaningful change. Digital marketing strategies, customer acquisition, and retention initiatives all take time to show significant results. They're not overnight solutions, but strategic investments in your business's future. 169 days gives these strategies enough time to gain momentum and deliver tangible results. But why not a round figure like 180 or 200 days? While round numbers can appear neat or convenient, they can also lead to procrastination or delay, encouraging the mentality of "I'll start on the next round number" - the next month, the next quarter, etc. The figure of 169 interrupts this pattern. It's immediate, prompting action here and now.

By the end of these 169 days, using the strategies and insights provided in this book, you will not only have seen substantial growth in your e-commerce sales but also acquired a wealth of knowledge and experience that will continue to drive your business's success long after this period. You will have established a robust foundation for your e-commerce business, characterized by effective digital marketing, a strong customer base, and a high conversion rate.

"4X Your E-commerce Sales in 169 Days" is your companion on this intense and rewarding journey. Now, without further ado, let's dive into the strategies that will propel your e-commerce business to new heights. Your 169 days to 4X your e-commerce sales start now!

⦸⦸⦸⦸

The most powerful product
you'll ever build is not what
you sell — it's who you
become in the process.

CHAPTER 2

THE READER'S JOURNEY

Your Transformation

Change is an integral part of any journey, and your journey through this book will be no different. Transformation is key here, both in terms of your e-commerce business and your own evolution as a business owner, leader, and strategist. This transformation doesn't happen overnight; it unfolds gradually, much like the 169-day journey that this book champions. Throughout, you'll gain strategies, insights, and a fresh perspective that will significantly impact how you view and operate your e-commerce business.

To embark on this transformational journey is to accept the challenges that come with it, and to learn, adapt, and grow in the process. Initially, you will gain an understanding of the basics of e-commerce - its fundamentals, types, and current landscape. As we delve deeper, you will be introduced to the power of digital marketing, the importance of SEO, the potential of PPC advertising, the benefits of content marketing, and the influential role of social media marketing.

As you absorb these lessons, you will begin to appreciate the strategic side of running an e-commerce business. You will realize that it's not just about having an online presence or selling products online; it's about carving out a unique space for your brand in the digital marketplace, creating value for your customers, and building strong, lasting relationships with them.

The focus will then shift to customer acquisition, retention, and conversion optimization. Here, you will learn about the importance of building a solid customer base and the various techniques that can help you achieve that. You will understand why customer retention is key to sustainable growth and how you can implement strategies to keep your customers coming back. You will also discover how to increase conversions and turn potential customers into actual buyers.

As we move forward, you'll follow a week-by-week action plan spanning 169 days, offering a structured and strategic roadmap to quadruple your sales. You will learn how to measure your success using Key Performance Indicators (KPIs) and how to overcome challenges that come your way.

By the end of this journey, not only will your e-commerce sales have experienced significant growth, but you will also have undergone a personal transformation. You will emerge as a more confident, knowledgeable, and strategic e-commerce business owner, equipped with the tools and insights necessary to navigate the dynamic world of e-commerce.

You will also be more resilient, having faced and overcome the various challenges thrown your way. This book, "4X Your E-commerce Sales in 169 Days," is not just about business transformation; it's about personal growth and evolution. The journey may be demanding, but the rewards at the end of these 169 days - and beyond - are worth it. The transformation starts now. Your transformation starts now.

Expected Outcomes

When you decided to embark on this journey through "4X Your E-commerce Sales in 169 Days," you likely had a set of expectations and outcomes in mind. This book aims to meet and exceed those expectations, guiding you towards a variety of transformative outcomes that extend far beyond mere profit maximization.

Knowledge Gain: One of the primary outcomes you'll get from this journey is a big boost in your e-commerce knowledge. You will dive into the various aspects of running a successful e-commerce business. This covers everything from understanding how e-commerce works to mastering SEO techniques, exploring effective content marketing strategies, unlocking the power of social media, and grasping the ins and outs of Pay-Per-Click (PPC) advertising. You'll also learn about the psychology of your customers – their behavior, needs, and desires – which is key to shaping your e-commerce strategy.

Strategic Expertise: With knowledge comes the power to strategize effectively. As you journey through this book, you'll move beyond just doing tactics to developing and implementing holistic, strategic plans. You'll start to understand why certain strategies work and others don't, and you'll start to see how different elements of your e-commerce business are interconnected. For example, you'll learn how the user experience on your website can affect your conversion rate, or how your SEO efforts can influence your site's organic traffic.

Enhanced Decision Making: As your knowledge and strategic skills grow, so will your ability to make informed decisions. You'll learn how to interpret and analyze data effectively, transforming raw numbers into valuable business insights. This skill will help you identify trends, spot opportunities, and make proactive changes that will drive your business growth. This enhanced decision-making capability will also allow you to minimize risk, optimize resource allocation, and ultimately, maximize profitability.

Growth in Sales: The application of the strategies and knowledge gained from this book should lead to a significant growth in sales, with a target to quadruple your sales figures by the end of the 169-day period. This isn't just about short-term sales increase, but also about setting the stage for consistent, long-term sales growth. You'll learn how to attract high-quality leads, improve conversion rates, and customer loyalty - all of which contribute to sustained sales growth.

Long-Term Sustainability: The ultimate outcome of this book goes beyond the 169 days. The goal is to equip you with the knowledge, skills, and strategies to make your e-commerce business not only profitable but also sustainable in the long term. By focusing on aspects like customer retention, brand building, and constant optimization, you'll be setting up your business for ongoing success.

In essence, as you progress through this book, you're not just working towards growing your e-commerce sales but also shaping a thriving, sustainable e-commerce business. The journey will be as rewarding as the destination.

⦸⦸⦸⦸

Before you learn the hacks,
understand the heartbeat.
Every click, cart, and conversion
starts with the basics.

CHAPTER 3

UNDERSTANDING E-COMMERCE BASICS

What is E-commerce?

At its core, e-commerce — or electronic commerce — refers to the buying and selling of goods or services over the internet. It encompasses a variety of commercial transactions across digital platforms.

However, the definition of e-commerce goes beyond this. It is a dynamic and rapidly evolving field that has fundamentally transformed the global business landscape.

Born out of technological advancements, e-commerce emerged as an exciting alternative to traditional brick-and-mortar businesses. It offers convenience, accessibility, and a virtually unlimited range of choices to consumers. For businesses, it is a cost-effective way to reach a global customer base without the need for physical stores or offices.

Each e-commerce model has its own unique dynamics, advantages, and challenges. Understanding these is essential as you shape your business strategy and align it with the model that best serves your objectives.

Additionally, e-commerce transactions can also be classified based on the nature of the goods or services being exchanged:

- **Physical Goods**: These are tangible products like clothes, appliances, books, or furniture that need to be physically delivered to the consumer once purchased.
- **Digital Goods:** Digital goods are intangible products in digital form and are typically delivered over the internet. This category includes software, digital media files like music, movies, or eBooks, and services like cloud storage or streaming platforms.
- **Services:** These include tasks or services performed by individuals or businesses in exchange for payment, such as consulting, tutoring, travel services, or professional services.

The internet is everywhere, and technology keeps growing fast. Because of this, e-commerce has become a global phenomenon all over the world, reaching into many different industries. Whether it's retail, finance, travel, or entertainment, e-commerce is now part of every business, making it easy to buy things with just a click or a swipe.

The Different Types of E-commerce

The world of e-commerce is not a monolith; rather, it's a varied landscape with different types of commerce models. These models are distinguished by the nature of the transactions that occur between different parties. It's critical for you to understand these different types of e-commerce since the strategies that you employ to drive sales growth may vary substantially depending on the specific model that your business operates within.

1. **Business-to-Consumer (B2C)**

   Business-to-Consumer e-commerce is the most well-known and straightforward type of e-commerce. In this model, a business sells goods and services directly to consumers over the internet. If you've ever bought a book from Amazon, a pair of shoes from Zappos, or a digital game from Steam, you've participated in B2C e-commerce.

The primary advantage of B2C is its potential for growth, thanks to the almost limitless online customer base. However, this sector can be highly competitive, with a need for high visibility and customer trust. Key success factors include user-friendly interfaces, efficient shipping and returns, effective customer service, and high-quality products.

2. **Business-to-Business (B2B)**

   While less visible to the average person, Business-to-Business e-commerce represents a significant portion of overall online transactions. Here, companies sell products and services to other businesses. Examples include a business buying software licenses for its employees' computers, or a restaurant purchasing ingredients from a wholesaler.

   B2B transactions are typically larger in volume and value compared to B2C transactions. Establishing trust and delivering excellent customer service is crucial here, as B2B customers often become long-term partners. Marketplaces like Alibaba and IndiaMART are great examples of platforms facilitating B2B transactions.

3. **Consumer-to-Consumer (C2C)**

   Consumer-to-Consumer e-commerce is another model where individual consumers sell goods and services to each other. Platforms like eBay and Etsy serve as intermediaries, providing the online marketplace for these transactions to occur.

   In C2C transactions, trust is of utmost importance, as both buyers and sellers are individuals. Therefore, robust systems for reviews, ratings, and dispute resolutions are critical for success. These platforms empower individuals to become entrepreneurs, contributing to the democratization of business.

4. **Consumer-to-Business (C2B)**

   The Consumer-to-Business model is a relatively new form of e-commerce. Here, consumers provide goods or services to businesses. This could involve a freelance web designer offering their services to businesses, or a customer selling a unique photo or design to a company to use in their marketing materials.

   C2B has emerged with the advent of the gig economy, with platforms like Upwork and Fiverr facilitating these types of transactions. It places individuals and businesses on equal footing, breaking down traditional business hierarchies.

   Understanding these four types of e-commerce will help you grasp the complexities of the e-commerce landscape. Each model has its own characteristics, opportunities, and challenges, and understanding these nuances is key to optimizing your strategy and maximizing your sales growth potential.

The E-commerce Landscape Today

To make the most of e-commerce and successfully boost your sales, a strong understanding of the current landscape is indispensable. This landscape is continually evolving, mainly because of technological advancements, shifts in consumer behavior, regulatory changes, and most recently, the impact of the global COVID-19 pandemic.

Growth and Market Size

Over the past decade, the e-commerce industry has witnessed substantial growth, with more and more retail transactions happening online. In 2022, global e-commerce sales reached an estimated $4.9 trillion, showing a clear sign of the industry's massive size. Projections suggest this figure will rise to $7.4 trillion by 2025, highlighting the immense potential available for businesses operating in the e-commerce sector.

Prominent Players

While Amazon and Alibaba often steal the spotlight, they're only a small part of the vast global e-commerce scene. The ecosystem is far more diverse, with a plethora of businesses ranging from retail giants to small-scale independent merchants. It spans across different sectors, including but not limited to, clothing, electronics, groceries, and services.

Additionally, essential supporting services are part of this landscape. Payment processors like PayPal and Stripe, delivery services such as UPS and FedEx, e-commerce platforms like Shopify and WooCommerce, and digital marketing and SEO agencies all play crucial roles in the ecosystem's success.

Trends in Consumer Behavior

The e-commerce landscape is strongly influenced by shifting consumer behavior trends. Today's consumers are digital natives who expect smooth, secure, and personalized shopping experiences. Geographical boundaries no longer limit their shopping behavior, as they regularly engage with brands from around the globe.

Consumer expectations have also evolved significantly. They prioritize sustainable brands and those that actively showcase social responsibility. Peer opinions matter more than ever, with online reviews and social proof becoming essential components of the buying process.

Impact of Technology

The tech-driven nature of e-commerce means that new technologies can drastically reshape the landscape. Today, mobile commerce, or m-commerce, accounts for a significant share of all e-commerce transactions. With consumers increasingly using smartphones for shopping, optimizing for mobile has become a necessity rather than a choice.

Other technologies like Artificial Intelligence (AI), Augmented Reality (AR), and Blockchain, are also disrupting the landscape. AI helps with personalization, trend prediction, and operational efficiency, while AR offers immersive shopping experiences. Blockchain promises to enhance supply chain transparency and security.

Payment and Logistics

Payments and logistics are two other critical aspects shaping the e-commerce landscape. Payment gateways have become more robust, offering secure transactions with multiple payment options, including digital wallets and cryptocurrencies.

Logistics have also improved, thanks to technology. Supply chain management, warehousing, and delivery have become more efficient with software solutions and automation, promising faster and more reliable order fulfillment.

Regulatory Environment and Pandemic Impact

Regulations governing data protection, consumer rights, and international trade play a vital role in the e-commerce landscape. While they aim to protect consumers and ensure fair competition, they often pose compliance challenges.

The COVID-19 pandemic significantly reshaped the landscape. As lockdowns pushed consumers online, businesses had to quickly adapt, with many moving online for the first time. This rapid acceleration of e-commerce is likely to have a lasting impact, even as the world returns to normal.

In conclusion, today's e-commerce landscape is a dynamic and swiftly evolving field, presenting both opportunities and challenges. Understanding its intricacies, including the influence of technology, consumer behavior trends, regulatory environment, and the impact of global events like the COVID-19 pandemic, is essential for businesses aiming to thrive in this competitive environment. With careful consideration and adaptation to these factors, businesses can effectively navigate the e-commerce terrain and capitalize on its vast potential for growth and success.

⦸⦸⦸⦸

The next era of economic power
won't be built in factories —
it will be clicked, shipped,
and scaled online.

CHAPTER 4

The Role of E-Commerce in Building a 5 Trillion-Dollar Economy

Introduction to the 5 Trillion-Dollar Economy

The term "5 trillion-dollar economy" has been making headlines, sparking debates among economists, policymakers, and business leaders worldwide. But what does it truly mean?

In essence, it refers to a nation's total economic output, or Gross Domestic Product (GDP), reaching or exceeding the colossal sum of 5 trillion dollars. The GDP, as a measure of a country's economic health, signifies the total value of all goods and services produced over a specific time period. To aspire towards a 5 trillion-dollar economy is to aim for significant economic growth and prosperity. The concept gained traction when countries like India declared this ambitious goal. However, it's not exclusive to any single nation. It serves as a benchmark that numerous economies, both emerging and developed, aim for to enhance their global economic stature.

Achieving a 5 trillion-dollar economy requires a multi-fold increase in production, consumption, investment, and exports. It demands job creation, innovation, and improvements across all sectors, be it manufacturing, agriculture, or services. It calls for a collective effort from all citizens, businesses, and government entities to sustain economic growth.

Within this vision, the role of e-commerce stands out as a potential game-changer. With the digital economy growing at an unprecedented rate, e-commerce has the power to contribute significantly to this ambitious target. By breaking down geographical barriers, it enables businesses to reach global customers, thereby boosting sales, profitability, and market reach.

E-commerce not only contributes directly to the GDP through increased business revenue but also indirectly fosters job creation and innovation. The industry's rapid growth drives demand for an array of ancillary services, from logistics to digital marketing, further fueling economic expansion.

In this chapter, we will explore in-depth the significant role that e-commerce plays in this economic transformation and how businesses like yours can ride this wave to multiply sales and contribute to the broader economic vision. Through understanding these dynamics, you will gain valuable insights to strategically position your business in the thriving e-commerce landscape and maximize your contribution to building a 5 trillion-dollar economy.

E-commerce: A Key Driver of Economic Growth

Now that we've introduced the concept of a 5 trillion-dollar economy, let's delve into the crucial role that e-commerce plays in this grand economic vision. E-commerce has completely transformed how businesses operate by providing a convenient, extensive, and cost-effective way to connect with customers worldwide. As a result, e-commerce has rapidly become a significant contributor to economic growth. E-commerce influences economic growth in several ways, starting with its direct impact on business revenue. By offering businesses an additional platform to reach out to consumers, e-commerce amplifies sales, thereby enhancing businesses' profitability and contributing to GDP growth.

But the impact of e-commerce extends beyond just direct revenue. It indirectly contributes to economic growth by fostering job creation across multiple sectors. These range from technical roles like web development and data analysis to operational roles in logistics and customer service. As more businesses shift or expand online, the demand for these roles increases, leading to job creation and a reduction in unemployment rates.

Furthermore, e-commerce drives innovation. The highly competitive nature of online businesses drives companies to constantly innovate, whether by improving user experience, adopting cutting-edge technologies, or developing novel business models. Such innovation not only benefits the individual business but also strengthens the overall economy.

In addition to this, e-commerce promotes international trade by breaking down geographical barriers, allowing businesses to reach consumers worldwide. This increase in exports helps balance trade deficits and propels economic growth.

E-commerce is also a critical driver for the growth of the digital economy, an increasingly significant part of the overall economy. The digital economy encompasses all economic activity that results from billions of daily online connections among people, businesses, devices, data, and processes. It's growing faster than the traditional economy, making it a key component of future economic growth.

In summary, e-commerce acts as a powerful engine for economic growth, directly and indirectly contributing to the vision of a 5 trillion-dollar economy. In the following sections, we'll explore how businesses can leverage this potential to multiply their sales and contribute to this ambitious economic goal.

Creating Opportunities for Businesses

E-commerce isn't just a crucial driver of economic growth at the macro level - it also presents a wealth of opportunities for businesses, regardless of their size. These opportunities can be a powerful catalyst for companies to achieve exponential growth and drive their contribution to a 5 trillion-dollar economy.

Firstly, e-commerce allows businesses to overcome the limitations of physical stores, such as geographical constraints, high operating costs, and limited working hours. An online platform offers unlimited reach, allowing businesses to tap into a global customer base. This global exposure not only increases potential sales but also opens the door to new partnerships, collaborations, and even foreign investment.

Secondly, e-commerce levels the playing field for small and medium-sized enterprises (SMEs). It provides SMEs with access to markets that were previously accessible only to larger corporations. By eliminating the need for extensive physical infrastructure and large upfront investments, it lowers barriers to entry and encourages entrepreneurship endeavors.

E-commerce also enables businesses to harness the power of data. With robust analytics tools, businesses can gain valuable insights into consumer behavior, preferences, and buying patterns. This data can drive targeted marketing strategies, optimized product offerings, and personalized customer experiences - all of which can significantly boost sales and customer loyalty.

In sum, e-commerce offers a plethora of opportunities for businesses to grow and thrive. By leveraging these opportunities, businesses can not only increase their sales but also contribute to the broader goal of a 5 trillion-dollar economy. The next sections will delve deeper into how to seize these opportunities and harness the power of e-commerce for exponential growth.

Boosting Employment and Entrepreneurship

A thriving e-commerce sector creates numerous job opportunities. As more businesses move online, there's a rising demand for an array of roles ranging from e-commerce strategists, website developers, digital marketers, to logistics managers. This growth also stimulates indirect job creation in related sectors such as packaging, delivery services, digital payment platforms, and customer service providers.

Each new job contributes to reducing unemployment rates, increasing purchasing power, and thus enhancing economic activity. The International Labour Organization (ILO) acknowledges e-commerce as a valuable source of job creation, particularly in developing economies, thereby contributing to economic growth and the grand vision of a 5 trillion-dollar economy.

Moreover, e-commerce fuels entrepreneurship by reducing entry barriers in terms of capital and infrastructure. It allows individuals and small enterprises to start businesses easily, leveraging platforms like Amazon and Etsy to reach global consumers. This has led to a rise in micro-enterprises and startups, fostering an entrepreneurial culture driven by innovation and self-employment. This dynamism not only boosts economic activity but also creates and distributes wealth, moving economies closer to the 5 trillion-dollar mark.

In the upcoming chapters, we will delve into how you, as an entrepreneur or a business, can leverage e-commerce to tap into this wealth of opportunities and 4X your sales. Furthermore, we will understand how this individual growth aligns with the bigger picture of economic prosperity.

Challenges and the Way Forward

While e-commerce offers promising prospects for economic growth and business expansion, it also brings a set of challenges that need to be addressed for optimal progress.

One significant challenge is the digital divide, in access to technology and internet connectivity, especially in rural and underprivileged communities. This inequality can limit the reach of e-commerce and its associated benefits.

Then there is the issue of cyber security. As digital transactions increase, so do the risks of data breaches, identity theft, and online fraud. It's crucial for businesses to prioritize cyber security to protect both themselves and their customers.

Regulatory hurdles also pose a significant challenge. As cross-border e-commerce grows, navigating the complex web of international trade laws, customs regulations, and tax compliances become a daunting task for many businesses.

However, with every challenge comes an opportunity for growth and innovation. To address the digital divide, there is a pressing need to invest in digital infrastructure and promote digital literacy. Such initiatives not only broaden the reach of e-commerce but also prepare the workforce for the digital economy.

For cyber security threats, businesses can leverage advanced technologies like AI and Blockchain for secure transactions. Additionally, a comprehensive legal and regulatory framework, both at the national and international level, is needed to address the regulatory challenges in e-commerce.

Lastly, continuous skill development is necessary to prepare the workforce for the changing job roles in the e-commerce era. This involves partnerships between businesses, educational institutions, and governments to align the skills of the workforce with the needs of the industry.

The road to leveraging e-commerce for a 5 trillion-dollar economy is challenging yet promising. By understanding and addressing these challenges, businesses can seize the opportunities presented by the e-commerce boom, significantly boosting their sales and contributing to the economic vision.

In the following chapters, we will delve into strategies to leverage e-commerce for business growth and how to navigate the challenges on the road to a 5 trillion-dollar economy.

⦸⦸⦸⦸

Big visions need strong systems. When entrepreneurs and enablers align, commerce becomes unstoppable.

CHAPTER 5

Government Initiatives: Facilitating Ease of Doing Business in the E-commerce Industry

Understanding 'Ease of Doing Business'

The term 'Ease of Doing Business' is likely familiar to you from business literature, news, and discussions, but what exactly does it mean?

Coined by the World Bank, 'Ease of Doing Business' measures how conducive a regulatory environment is for starting and operating a business in any country. It evaluates regulations directly impacting businesses and does so not just in the nation's largest business cities. The World Bank compiles this data to rank countries based on the ease of doing business..

Ease of Doing Business affects many factors, from attracting foreign investment to fostering domestic entrepreneurial talent. An environment with greater ease of doing business often witnesses higher economic activity, resulting in a prosperous and vibrant economy.

In the world of the e-commerce industry, 'Ease of Doing Business' relates to the friendliness of the regulatory environment for launching and managing an online business. This includes factors like ease of starting a business, obtaining necessary permits and licenses, getting credit, protecting minority investors, paying taxes, enforcing contracts, and resolving insolvency issues.

For the e-commerce sector to thrive and for businesses to fully exploit the opportunities it presents, it is imperative that the 'Ease of Doing Business' is high. Governments worldwide recognize this and are implementing reforms to streamline regulations, improve infrastructure, and provide support to businesses, particularly in the digital domain.

These initiatives are critical in achieving the dual goal of individual business growth and wider economic prosperity. In the sections to follow, we will explore some of these initiatives and how they facilitate business growth in the e-commerce sector, contributing to the journey towards a 5 trillion-dollar economy.

Government Role in E-commerce

In the fast-changing landscape of e-commerce, the role of government goes beyond just regulation. They also act as facilitators, supporters, and sometimes even participants in the e-commerce system.

As a regulator, the government frames laws and guidelines to ensure fair competition, protect consumer rights, and prevent malpractices in the e-commerce sector. It sets standards for data privacy, establishes rules for online transactions, and enforces anti-trust laws to prevent the formation of monopolies.

As an enabler, the government works to make it easier for e-commerce businesses to succeed. This involves implementing policies that facilitate 'Ease of Doing Business', like simplifying business registration processes, easing tax regulations, and providing financial aid or incentives to startups. They also invest in improving infrastructure, like better internet access, stronger cyber security, and teaching people how to use digital tools.

Sometimes, the government also acts as a participant in the e-commerce ecosystem. For instance, government-run e-marketplaces connect vendors with government buyers, fostering transparency and efficiency in public procurement processes.

Government initiatives in e-commerce play a vital role in shaping the industry's growth and its contribution to the economy. By creating a favorable business environment, safeguarding interests, and fostering innovation and competitiveness, governments can significantly impact the journey towards a 5 trillion-dollar economy.

In the upcoming sections, we will delve deeper into some key government initiatives aimed at boosting e-commerce and how businesses can take advantage of them to grow and succeed.

Key Government Initiatives

Governments worldwide have implemented a range of initiatives to boost the e-commerce sector. These initiatives aim to simplify business operations, encourage entrepreneurship, and ensure fair and transparent digital marketplaces. Let's look at some key initiatives that have significantly enhanced the 'Ease of Doing Business' in e-commerce.

This reduces paperwork and saves time, making it easier for businesses to start operations.

- **E-commerce Regulatory Frameworks:** Governments have established comprehensive regulatory frameworks for e-commerce. These regulations address important issues such as data protection, consumer rights, competition, and taxation. By providing clear and comprehensive regulations, governments provide a stable environment for e-commerce businesses to operate.
- **Financial Support and Incentives:** Many governments provide financial support to e-commerce businesses in the form of grants, loans, and tax incentives. These measures help reduce the financial burden on businesses, especially startups, and encourage entrepreneurship in the e-commerce sector.
- **Investment in Infrastructure:** Governments play a crucial role in developing the necessary infrastructure for e-commerce. This includes improving internet connectivity, establishing secure digital payment systems, and developing efficient logistics and delivery networks.
- **Capacity Building Initiatives:** Governments also run programs to boost skills and knowledge in the e-commerce sector. This includes providing training programs to develop digital skills, fostering research and innovation in e-commerce, and promoting digital literacy among the population.
- These initiatives not only make it easier for businesses to operate in the e-commerce sector but also help build a competitive e-commerce ecosystem. As we move through this book, we will look at how businesses can leverage these initiatives to scale their operations and achieve exponential growth.

Impact of These Initiatives

Improved Business Environment

- **Enhanced Trust:** Clear regulations around data protection and consumer rights have helped increase consumer trust in online transactions. This has led to an increased adoption of e-commerce by consumers, contributing to the sector's growth.
- **Increased Access to Capital:** Financial support and incentives from the government have made capital more accessible to e-commerce businesses, especially startups and SMEs. This has enabled these businesses to invest in innovation and expansion, driving growth in the sector.
- **Infrastructure Development:** Government-led infrastructure development has made it possible for e-commerce to reach a wider population. Improved internet connectivity has increased the potential customer base for e-commerce businesses. At the same time, secure digital payment systems and efficient logistics networks have made online transactions more convenient and reliable.
- **Skilled Workforce:** Government capacity building initiatives have helped create a workforce that is equipped with the necessary digital skills. This has not only created employment opportunities but has also ensured that e-commerce businesses have access to the talent they need.

In conclusion, these initiatives have not only improved the ease of doing business in the e-commerce sector but have also helped build a strong foundation for its sustainable growth. Businesses that are aware of and can effectively leverage these initiatives are likely to experience success in their e-commerce ventures, potentially achieving up to 4X sales growth. In the upcoming chapters, we will discuss in detail how businesses can achieve this growth by taking advantage of the favorable business environment.

Future Government Support

Government support for the e-commerce industry is an ongoing process, as the needs and challenges of the industry evolve with technology and market dynamics. Therefore, it's crucial to have an idea of what future government support for the e-commerce industry might look like.

One significant area of focus for future government support is likely to be technology and innovation. As technologies such as artificial intelligence, blockchain, and augmented reality become more crucial in e-commerce, governments may launch initiatives to promote research and development in these areas. This could include funding for tech startups, partnerships between universities and businesses, and training programs to develop skills in these technologies.

Digital infrastructure will continue to be a critical area of government focus. This could involve initiatives to improve internet connectivity, particularly in rural and underserved areas, and to strengthen cybersecurity against online threats.

Governments are also likely to focus on creating a fair e-commerce ecosystem. This could involve initiatives to ensure that small and medium-sized enterprises (SMEs) can compete effectively with large e-commerce platforms, and that the benefits of e-commerce are shared widely across society.

Lastly, with the increasing global emphasis on sustainability, we can expect government regulations and incentives promoting environmentally friendly practices in e-commerce. This could range from regulations on packaging and delivery, to incentives for businesses that reduce their carbon footprint.

In the future, government support will continue to be a significant factor in the growth and development of the e-commerce industry. Understanding the likely direction of this support can help businesses align their strategies and operations to make the most of the opportunities that arise. In the subsequent chapters of this book, we will explore some of these opportunities and provide guidance on how to leverage them for 4X sales growth.

⦸⦸⦸⦸

Avoiding compliance may save costs today, but it costs far more tomorrow. Smart entrepreneurs don't gamble with peace of mind.

CHAPTER 6

NAVIGATING TAXATION & COMPLIANCE IN E-COMMERCE

Understanding E-commerce Taxation

Taxation is a critical aspect of any business, and e-commerce is no exception. As online transactions become more common, understanding e-commerce taxation becomes increasingly important.

E-commerce taxation is about applying tax laws to transactions conducted over the internet. However, the unique characteristics of e-commerce - including digital goods, cross-border transactions, and the role of intermediaries - make taxation in this sector complex.

Different countries have different approaches to e-commerce taxation, and it can be broadly classified into two categories: Direct and Indirect Taxes.

Direct taxes, such as corporate income tax, are usually based on an e-commerce business's profits. The rules depend on the business's legal structure, physical presence, and where it earns its income.

Indirect taxes, such as Goods and Services Tax (GST), Value Added Tax (VAT), or sales tax, are typically levied on the sale of goods and services. In the context of e-commerce, these taxes can apply to digital products, online services, and physical goods sold online. Again, the rules can vary depending on the location of the seller, the buyer, and the nature of the goods or services.

In addition to these taxes, e-commerce businesses might also need to consider import and export duties if they are involved in cross-border transactions.

In the upcoming sections of this chapter, we will delve deeper into the various aspects of e-commerce taxation and provide guidance on how to navigate this complex area. We will also discuss the importance of compliance in the e-commerce sector and provide tips on how to ensure your business meets all its legal and regulatory obligations.

Compliance Regulations in E-commerce

Compliance is a crucial factor in running a successful e-commerce business. Compliance regulations in e-commerce cover a wide range of aspects, from data protection and consumer rights to payment regulations and advertising standards.

Non-compliance can lead to fines, legal issues, and damage to your business reputation, making it a top priority for any e-commerce business.

- **Data Protection and Privacy:** With the increased digitization of consumer data, regulations around data protection and privacy have become more stricter. Businesses are required to adhere to data protection laws such as GDPR in Europe or CCPA in California, which specify how consumer data should be collected, stored, and used. Compliance with these regulations is critical in building consumer trust and avoiding heavy penalties.

- **Consumer Protection Laws:** These laws are in place to ensure fair trade, competition, and accurate information in the marketplace. They protect consumers from fraud, false advertising, and unfair terms. An e-commerce business must understand and adhere to the specific consumer protection laws applicable in their operating region.
- **Payment Regulations:** These regulations cover aspects like security standards for card transactions, rules around refunds, and handling of customer payment data. Failure to comply with payment regulations can lead to financial loss and damage to your business's reputation.
- **Advertising Standards:** These standards ensure that advertisements are honest and truthful, not misleading, and respectful of the diversity in a society. They apply to all forms of advertising, including online advertisements, social media posts, and influencer marketing.

As the landscape of e-commerce evolves, so do the regulations that govern it. Keeping up with these changes and ensuring compliance is not only a legal necessity but also a best practice that contributes to the smooth operation and success of your e-commerce business. The following sections of this chapter will delve into the practical aspects of ensuring compliance and navigating the complex web of e-commerce regulations.

International Tax and Compliance Considerations

When it comes to e-commerce, businesses often face challenges related to international taxation and compliance. International taxation for e-commerce businesses generally refers to the tax obligations that arise when businesses operate in multiple countries or when goods and services are sold across borders. This includes corporate taxes imposed by different countries, cross-border sales taxes, customs duties, and digital service taxes. Each country has its own tax regulations that apply to e-commerce. These could be based on factors like the physical presence of the business, the location of the server, the place of payment, or the delivery of goods or services. Some countries may have treaties with others to avoid double taxation, but the rules can be complex and may vary widely. Likewise, international compliance can be complex. This can include compliance with foreign laws and regulations related to data protection, consumer rights, advertising standards, and payment regulations.

For instance, a U.S. based e-commerce company selling to customers in the European Union needs to comply with the EU's General Data Protection Regulation (GDPR).

Moreover, businesses operating internationally need to be aware of international trade laws, such as export control regulations and anti-bribery laws. Violations of these laws can lead to substantial penalties and reputational damage. It's also important to consider that non-compliance with tax laws and regulations can not only lead to financial penalties but also operational disruptions, such as goods being held at customs.

Navigating international tax and compliance can be challenging, but it's an essential part of running a successful e-commerce business. As such, it is recommended to seek professional advice and use automated tools wherever possible to ensure compliance and keep up with changes in regulations. In the next sections, we will explore these strategies and provide practical tips to help you manage international tax and compliance effectively.

Embracing the Digital Frontier: The Impact of Recognizing Virtual Place of Business in India

In a significant shift in India's taxation and regulatory framework, the recognition of the 'virtual place of business' concept marks a new era for e-commerce and digital businesses. This recognition is a testament to the growing digital economy of India and the need to align existing frameworks with current realities.

This shift acknowledges the unique operational models of digital businesses, which may not have a traditional physical presence but have substantial virtual footprints. For these businesses, a virtual place of business allows them to be recognized as entities operating within the country, even if their operations are entirely online.

The Indian Government's decision to recognize virtual places of business has brought about notable changes in the tax and compliance landscape for e-commerce businesses. The concept of 'virtual presence' has become crucial for determining tax liability under the Goods and Services Tax (GST) laws, making the taxation process more straightforward and transparent.

This change goes beyond taxation. For e-commerce, it provides legal legitimacy, ensuring that online activities, transactions, and regulations are recognized by law.

Furthermore, the compliance requirements for businesses have been updated to reflect this concept. Virtual businesses are now subject to the same regulations that govern traditional businesses, including data protection laws, consumer protection regulations, and advertising standards. As a result, these businesses must ensure that their operations are in line with these rules to avoid legal repercussions.

In essence, the recognition of virtual places of business has provided e-commerce businesses with a clearer roadmap to navigate taxation and compliance in India. The challenge now is for businesses to adapt and integrate these challenges into their operations, keeping up with the evolving regulatory landscape. The following sections will provide a comprehensive guide on how to adapt to these changes, focusing on practical strategies and compliance best practices in the age of digital business operations.

Addressing the Challenges of Virtual Place of Business in India

Although recognizing the concept of the 'virtual place of business' has brought several advantages, it also presents unique challenges for e-commerce businesses. One significant challenge is determining the 'place of supply' for tax purposes. Given the borderless nature of the internet, e-commerce transactions can happen anywhere in India or abroad, which can complicate the process of identifying the location of supply for GST.

The Indian tax authorities have issued guidance on this issue, stating that the place of supply for online sales should generally be considered the location where the goods are delivered or services are . However, for certain services like online advertising or data hosting, determining the place of supply can be more complex.

Another challenge is ensuring data protection and privacy compliance. Since virtual businesses often handle sensitive customer data, they must comply with India's data protection laws, including the Personal Data Protection Act. This involves implementing appropriate security measures, obtaining consent for data collection and use, and ensuring that cross-border data transfers are conducted in a compliant manner.

Moreover, compliance with consumer protection regulations is crucial. As per the Consumer Protection (E-Commerce) Rules, e-commerce entities operating in India must provide accurate product information, establish a grievance redressal mechanism, and avoid unfair trade practices. Violations of these rules can lead to penalties and reputational damage.

In the next sections, we will delve deeper into these challenges and explore effective strategies to address them. From understanding the nuances of GST for e-commerce to ensuring data privacy compliance, we will provide you with a roadmap to navigate the complexities of operating a virtual place of business in India.

Solutions and Strategies for Virtual Place of Business Compliance

Finding solutions and strategies for complying with regulations in the virtual business world might seem overwhelming, but with the right approach, businesses can navigate the landscape effectively and minimize risks. Here are some steps to consider:

1. **Understanding Tax Laws:** The first step is to grasp the tax laws that apply to e-commerce. Seeking guidance from tax experts and staying updated with GST notifications and circulars can provide valuable insights.
2. **Automating Tax Compliance:** Using software solutions can streamline tax compliance processes. These tools can calculate GST on e-commerce transactions, generate invoices with accurate tax rates, and prepare tax returns. This automation helps reduce the chances of errors and ensures compliance.

3. **Data Protection Compliance:** Data protection is crucial, so businesses should conduct regular audits to ensure compliance. Implementing strong data security measures and providing clear privacy policies to customers are essential steps. Employing a Data Protection Officer (DPO) or seeking expert advice can further ensure compliance with data protection laws.
4. **Consumer Protection Regulations:** It's vital to align operations with consumer protection rules. This involves providing accurate product information, addressing customer complaints promptly, and maintaining transparency in all operations.

By following these steps, businesses can navigate the regulatory landscape effectively and ensure compliance with laws and regulations governing virtual business operations.

In essence, navigating the compliance landscape for virtual places of business involves a combination of staying informed, leveraging technology, and seeking expert advice. The journey might seem challenging, but with the right strategies, businesses can thrive in the digital economy of India.

Maintaining Tax and Compliance Records

In the evolving landscape of e-commerce, maintaining accurate tax and compliance records is a critical task that businesses cannot afford to overlook. These records serve as proof of your business's adherence to India's taxation laws and regulations, and they play an integral role in your dealings with government entities and tax authorities. In essence, the records you maintain are the lifeblood of your business's tax and compliance strategy.

Primarily, tax records consist of financial documents that show the tax you have collected, the tax you have paid, and any tax deductions or credits you've claimed. These records include sales invoices, purchase invoices, bank statements, expense receipts, tax payment receipts, and various tax returns.

Compliance records, on the other hand, may include a wider range of documents related to your business operations. These could encompass anything from data protection policies and records of data processing activities to evidence of compliance with consumer protection laws, such as records of customer complaints and their resolution.

The key to effective record keeping is a well-organized system that allows you to store and retrieve records easily. Given the volume of transactions and activities in an e-commerce business, digital record keeping has become a necessity. Numerous software solutions and cloud-based services are available that offer secure, efficient, and compliant ways to manage your records.

These digital systems can also provide easy access to historical data, generate detailed reports, and even automate aspects of record keeping, such as reconciling bank statements or tracking GST on sales. Embracing these technological solutions can significantly streamline the process of maintaining your tax and compliance records.

The other side of record keeping is ensuring that you retain these records for the required period. As per the GST law in India, businesses are required to maintain their records for at least six years from the due date of filing the annual return for the relevant year.

In essence, maintaining tax and compliance records is not merely a regulatory requirement, but a strategic necessity for every e-commerce business. It allows for smoother audits, promotes transparency, helps in strategic decision-making, and, most importantly, ensures peace of mind in knowing that you are on the right side of the law. In the next sections, we will explore how you can optimize and automate your record-keeping processes to make them more effective and less time-consuming.

Future Trends in E-commerce Taxation and Compliance

As e-commerce continues to evolve in India, it's critical for businesses to keep a keen eye on the future trends in taxation and compliance. These trends are indicative of the future policy direction and can have a significant impact on how e-commerce businesses operate.

One of the key trends to watch is the increased use of digital technologies by the tax authorities. The Indian government has made significant strides towards digitalization of tax administration, with initiatives like the e-assessment scheme and the e-invoicing system. These digital platforms are streamlining tax compliance, minimizing manual intervention, and reducing the scope for errors and discrepancies.

Another important trend is the continuous evolution of laws and regulations related to data privacy and consumer protection. As more and more businesses shift online and as consumers become increasingly aware of their rights, the government is likely to introduce more robust measures to protect consumer interests and data privacy.

Furthermore, as e-commerce expands to cover new types of services and products, the tax and regulatory framework will need to adapt accordingly. We can anticipate new norms and regulations to address the tax implications of emerging technologies and business models, such as cryptocurrencies, NFTs, and the sharing economy.

Another major trend is the global shift towards greater tax transparency and cooperation between nations to prevent tax evasion. This might affect how e-commerce businesses handle international transactions and deal with issues like transfer pricing and double taxation.

In the future, there may also be significant changes in how taxes are imposed on digital services. Currently, GST is applied based on the location of the supplier, but there is a growing global trend towards applying taxes based on the location of the consumer. India is already observing this in the case of cross-border digital services through the 'Equalization Levy,' and we may see a similar approach being extended to other areas of e-commerce.

In India, e-commerce taxation and compliance is continuously evolving, driven by technological advancements, changing consumer behaviors, and the dynamic nature of the e-commerce industry. It's crucial for e-commerce businesses to stay updated with these trends, adapt to the changes, and strategize for the future. In the subsequent chapters, we will dive deeper into the practical aspects of these trends and provide actionable insights to help you navigate the future of e-commerce taxation and compliance.

Avoiding compliance may save costs today, but it costs far more tomorrow. Smart entrepreneurs don't gamble with peace of mind.

CHAPTER 7

THE POWER OF DIGITAL MARKETING

Introduction to Digital Marketing

In today's business landscape, the influence of digital marketing is undeniable. As commerce increasingly shifts to the digital world, this dynamic marketing approach has become essential for e-commerce success. Through strategic digital marketing, businesses can connect with their target audience, boost brand visibility, and achieve substantial sales growth.

Digital marketing involves promoting products or services through digital channels to reach consumers. These channels could be owned media like your website or email list, earned media through organic reach and reputation management, or paid media through ads. In essence, digital marketing encompasses any effort to promote your business online.

What makes digital marketing stand out is its vast reach, precise targeting, and adaptability. With the rise of internet connectivity across India, digital marketing empowers businesses to tap into a wide demographic that was previously unreachable. No longer are businesses limited by geographical boundaries; the digital marketplace is worldwide, thus exponentially expanding the potential customer base.

Furthermore, digital marketing enables businesses to target customers with unparalleled precision. Techniques such as Search Engine Optimization (SEO), Pay-Per-Click (PPC) advertising, social media marketing, and email marketing, among others, enable marketers to tailor their strategies based on detailed demographic data, consumer behavior, interests, and various other parameters.

One of the most attractive features of digital marketing is its adaptability. Unlike traditional marketing that often requires significant upfront investment and rigid planning, digital marketing campaigns can be adjusted in real-time based on performance metrics. This flexibility allows businesses to experiment with different strategies , learn from analytics, and continuously refine their approach to gain the best results.

In the context of e-commerce, the strategic application of digital marketing can yield remarkable benefits, including attracting quality website traffic, improving product visibility, fostering customer engagement, and significantly amplifying sales.

However, harnessing the power of digital marketing comes with its challenges. The digital marketing environment is diverse, dynamic, and ever-evolving, with new platforms, strategies, and trends continually emerging. It can be overwhelming for businesses, especially new entrants, to navigate this landscape and keep pace with the continual evolution.

Throughout this chapter, we will delve deeper into the fascinating world of digital marketing. We will examine the key components that underpin a successful digital marketing strategy, discuss the latest techniques and trends shaping the digital marketing landscape, and offer practical tips to help you optimize your digital marketing efforts. Whether you're an established e-commerce business or a newcomer to the digital market, the insights shared in this chapter aim to equip you with a solid foundation to harness the full potential of digital marketing and significantly escalate your e-commerce sales.

SEO for E-commerce

SEO, or Search Engine Optimization, is a foundational pillar of digital marketing. It is the process of improving the quality and quantity of website traffic by increasing the visibility of a website or a webpage to users of a web search engine. For e-commerce businesses, mastering SEO is fundamental to securing a digital presence that not only reaches but also engages and converts the vast online audience.

The primary function of SEO in the context of e-commerce is to enable your business's website to rank higher in search engine results pages (SERPs). High rankings can lead to increased visibility among potential customers, resulting in more organic (non-paid) traffic to your website, and eventually, more conversions.

A well-rounded e-commerce SEO strategy covers various aspects. It starts with understanding your audience and identifying relevant keywords they might use to search for your products or services. These keywords should then be integrated into your website content, meta tags, URLs, and alt texts in a manner that feels organic and improves user experience.

Another crucial facet of e-commerce SEO involves ensuring that your website architecture is search-engine-friendly. This entails having a clean, user-friendly site structure, employing SEO-friendly URLs, and implementing a comprehensive internal linking strategy.

Equally important is the technical health of your website. Slow loading speeds, broken links, or mobile unfriendliness can significantly harm your SEO performance. Regular technical SEO audits can help identify and fix these issues, ensuring that search engines can easily crawl and index your website.

Moreover, the quality of your content plays a crucial role in SEO. Creating engaging, valuable content not only improves the user experience but also signals to search engines that your website is a reliable source of information. This can significantly enhance your search engine rankings.

Off-page SEO, which involves activities outside of your own website, is another vital component of an e-commerce SEO strategy. This includes earning backlinks from reputable websites, which can boost your site's authority in the eyes of search engines, and managing online reviews and ratings, which can significantly influence your SEO performance and overall online reputation.

In the context of e-commerce, product pages require particular attention. These should be optimized with high-quality product images, detailed and unique product descriptions, and user-generated content like reviews and ratings. Last but not least, tracking and analysis are essential to any successful SEO strategy. Regular monitoring of your website's SEO performance using tools like Google Analytics or Search Console can provide valuable insights into what's working and what needs improvement. SEO is a long-term process, and constant monitoring, testing, and tweaking are necessary to stay ahead of the competition and keep up with ever-evolving search engine algorithms.

In conclusion, SEO is a powerful tool that can significantly improve your e-commerce business's online visibility, drive organic traffic, and ultimately increase sales. However, it requires a strategic approach, meticulous execution, and constant monitoring and optimization. With the right SEO practices in place, you can harness the power of search engines to fuel your e-commerce growth.

PPC Advertising

Pay-Per-Click (PPC) advertising, another pivotal element of the digital marketing arsenal, is a model of internet marketing where advertisers pay a fee each time one of their ads is clicked. Essentially, it's a way of buying visits to your site, rather than attempting to "earn" those visits organically through SEO. When properly executed, PPC advertising can provide your e-commerce business with a substantial return on investment.

PPC advertising can serve multiple purposes: it can help increase brand visibility, drive traffic to your website, boost product sales, or generate leads. Unlike many other forms of marketing, PPC advertising allows you to reach people who are actively searching for products or services similar to what your e-commerce business offers.

The most popular platform for PPC advertising is Google Ads, previously known as Google AdWords. Google Ads operate on an auction system, which takes place every time a user performs a keyword search. Advertisers choose a set of keywords related to their business offerings, create an advertisement that will appear in the search engine results page (SERP), and bid on a price they're willing to pay for each click.

The position of your ad is determined by your bid amount and your ad's Quality Score, a measure of the quality of your ads, keywords, and landing pages. Higher Quality Scores can lead to lower prices and better ad positions. However, Google Ads isn't the only platform for PPC advertising. Other platforms, such as Bing Ads, Amazon Advertising, and social media platforms like Facebook and Instagram, also offer PPC advertising opportunities. Each platform has its unique set of benefits and is suited for different types of e-commerce businesses.

For instance, Amazon advertising is an excellent choice for e-commerce businesses that sell physical products. Meanwhile, Facebook and Instagram ads can be beneficial for businesses aiming to build a strong brand presence and engage with their audience on a deeper level.

Creating a successful PPC campaign requires careful planning and execution. It starts with understanding your business goals and your target audience. Once you have that clear, you can conduct keyword research, create compelling ad copies, and design landing pages that convert. Remember, the goal of PPC advertising is not just to drive traffic but to attract potential customers who are likely to convert. Therefore, the relevancy of your ads, the quality of your landing pages, and the overall user experience are all crucial for the success of your PPC campaign.

Monitoring and optimizing your PPC campaigns is an ongoing process. You should regularly review your campaign performance, experiment with different ad copies and landing pages, adjust your bids, and refine your targeting to improve your return on investment.

Tools like Google Analytics and Google Ads' built-in analytics can provide valuable insights into your campaign performance and help you make data-driven decisions.

In summary, PPC advertising can be a highly effective marketing tool for e-commerce businesses, provided it is implemented strategically. With the right approach, PPC can help you reach your target audience at the right time, increase your online visibility, drive qualified traffic to your website, and ultimately boost your e-commerce sales.

Content Marketing

Content Marketing is a strategic marketing approach centered around creating, publishing, and distributing valuable, relevant, and consistent content to attract and retain a clearly-defined audience. It involves educating your customers about your products and industry without selling directly to them. The ultimate goal of content marketing is to drive profitable customer action.

For e-commerce businesses, content marketing can be a potent tool for attracting traffic, building trust with potential customers, boosting SEO performance, and establishing your brand as an authority in your industry. A well-planned content marketing strategy involves understanding your target audience's needs and preferences, and creating content that meets these needs. It includes different forms of content, such as blog posts, how-to guides, video content, podcasts, infographics, case studies, webinars, and more. Your content should provide value to the reader, helping them solve a problem, learn something new, or make an informed decision. By doing so, you can build a strong relationship with your audience, fostering trust and loyalty towards your brand.

Effective content marketing is more than just creating and sharing content. It also involves content promotion, ensuring your content reaches the right audience at the right time. This can be achieved through various channels such as social media, email marketing, SEO, paid advertising, and more.

In e-commerce, content marketing can serve multiple purposes. It can help:

- **Educate Customers:** Create in-depth product guides, how-to videos, or comparison articles to help customers understand your products better and how they can benefit from them.
- **Boost SEO:** By creating high-quality, SEO-friendly content, you can improve your website's search engine rankings and attract more organic traffic.
- **Build Trust and Authority:** By sharing expert insights, tips, and advice, you can establish your brand as an authority in your industry, building trust with your audience.
- **Nurture Leads:** Through content like newsletters, personalized emails, and educational webinars, you can nurture potential customers, moving them down the sales funnel and closer to making a purchase.
- **Improve Customer Retention:** By consistently providing valuable content, you can keep your existing customers engaged and foster long-term customer relationships.

Just like other digital marketing strategies, content marketing requires constant monitoring and optimization. It's crucial to measure your content performance using key metrics like website traffic, time spent on page, social shares, conversions, etc., to understand what's working and what's not.

In summary, content marketing can significantly enhance your e-commerce marketing efforts. By providing valuable content consistently, you can attract, engage, and retain your audience, thereby driving more traffic, boosting conversions, and increasing customer loyalty.

Social Media Marketing

In the digital era, Social Media Marketing (SMM) is an indispensable tool for e-commerce businesses. It leverages platforms such as Facebook, Instagram, Twitter, LinkedIn, Pinterest, and YouTube to connect with your audience, build your brand, increase sales, and drive website traffic. By harnessing the power of social media, businesses can engage their audience in a more personalized and interactive way.

Successful social media marketing begins with a comprehensive strategy. Your strategy should outline your goals (increasing brand awareness, driving traffic, boosting conversions, etc.), target audience, content themes, posting frequency, and key performance metrics. Each social media platform has its own unique features, audience demographics, and content preferences. Therefore, your approach should be tailored to each platform.

For instance, Instagram is ideal for visually appealing content and lifestyle branding, while LinkedIn is suited for B2B marketing and professional networking.

Content is at the heart of social media marketing. Sharing high-quality, engaging content that resonates with your audience is key to driving engagement and conversions. This could be in the form of product photos, how-to videos, user-generated content, blog posts, infographics, contests, polls, live Q&As, and more.

The power of social media also lies in its ability to foster two-way communication. Engage with your audience by responding to comments, direct messages, and customer inquiries in a timely manner. This can help build a strong relationship with your audience, foster trust, and enhance your brand's online reputation. In addition to organic social media marketing, most platforms also offer paid advertising options. Social media advertising allows you to target your ads to a specific audience based on demographics, interests, behaviors, and more. This can help increase your reach, attract potential customers, and boost conversions.

Remember, though, that the key to successful social media advertising is to create ads that don't feel like ads. Your ads should provide value, be visually appealing, and blend seamlessly with the user's feed.

Lastly, tracking and analyzing your social media performance is critical to optimizing your strategy. Use platform-specific insights and tools like Google Analytics to track your key performance metrics such as engagement rate, follower growth, reach, impressions, click-through rate, conversions, and more. This data can provide valuable insights into what's working, what's not, and how you can improve your social media marketing strategy.

Email Marketing

Email marketing involves sending targeted emails to prospects and customers. This could include promotional emails, newsletters, cart abandonment reminders, and personalized product recommendations. Email is a powerful tool for nurturing leads and encouraging repeat purchases.

Affiliate Marketing

In affiliate marketing, other people (affiliates) promote your products and earn a commission on any sales they generate. It's a cost-effective technique because you only pay for results.

Referral Programs

Referral programs involve incentivizing your existing customers to refer their friends. This could be in the form of discounts, free products, or other rewards. Referrals can be a powerful tool because people tend to trust recommendations from friends.

In summary, social media marketing offers a powerful way for e-commerce businesses to reach their target audience, build brand awareness, drive traffic, and increase sales. By crafting a solid strategy, sharing engaging content, interacting with your audience, and leveraging paid advertising, you can harness the power of social media to supercharge your e-commerce sales.

Customer acquisition isn't about how many people you reach. It's about how many come back.

CHAPTER 8

Customer Acquisition: Building a Solid Customer Base

Understanding Customer Acquisition

Customer acquisition is the process of persuading a consumer to purchase a company's goods or services. In e-commerce, it involves various strategies and tactics to attract first-time buyers to your online store. It's a crucial part of your e-commerce business because without a steady flow of new customers, your business will not grow.

It's important to understand that customer acquisition is more than just making a sale. It's about creating a relationship with the customer that encourages repeat business and fosters customer loyalty.

In the world of e-commerce, customer acquisition involves a series of steps, often referred to as the "customer acquisition funnel" or "sales funnel." These steps include:

- **Awareness:** Potential customers become aware of your brand through various marketing channels like search engines, social media, content marketing, and advertising.

- **Interest:** They start to show interest in your products or services by visiting your website, subscribing to your email list, or following you on social media.
- **Consideration:** They start to consider making a purchase, comparing your offerings with competitors, and reading customer reviews.
- **Conversion:** They decide to make a purchase and become a customer.
- **Retention:** Through effective customer service and engagement strategies, you aim to retain the customer, encouraging repeat purchases and fostering customer loyalty.

To be successful in customer acquisition, it's important to understand your target audience — their needs, preferences, buying behaviors, and pain points. This will help you craft a tailored marketing and sales strategy that resonates with them.

Creating buyer personas can be a useful strategy. A buyer persona represents your ideal customer, based on market research and real data about your existing customers. It helps you understand who you are targeting, what they are looking for, what kind of messaging will appeal to them, and where to find them.

The cost of acquiring a new customer — often referred to as Customer Acquisition Cost (CAC) — is a critical metric for e-commerce businesses. It's calculated by dividing the total cost spent on acquisition by the number of new customers acquired during the period the money was spent.

Keeping CAC as low as possible is crucial because the lower your CAC, the higher your profit margins. That's why effective and cost-efficient marketing strategies are crucial.

Customer acquisition is not a one-size-fits-all process. What works for one business may not work for another. It's important to experiment with different strategies, track your performance, and continuously optimize your approach.

In the next sections, we'll delve deeper into different customer acquisition strategies and techniques, from digital marketing to referral programs, to help you attract more customers and grow your e-commerce business.

Building a Customer Acquisition Strategy

A well-defined customer acquisition strategy lays the groundwork for your e-commerce business growth. It determines how you attract new customers, the tactics you use, and how you will track and measure success. An effective strategy also takes into account your business goals, target audience, unique value proposition, and budget.

The first step in building a customer acquisition strategy is setting clear, measurable goals. Your goals might be to increase website traffic, boost conversions, expand into a new market segment, or improve customer retention. It's crucial to align these goals with your broader business objectives.

The second step is understanding your target audience. As we discussed earlier, creating detailed buyer personas can help here. Consider your audience's demographics, behaviors, needs, and motivations. Also, understand their online habits — which websites do they frequently visit? Which social media platforms do they use? What type of content do they engage with?

Next, identify your Unique Value Proposition (UVP). Your UVP is what sets you apart from the competition. It's the unique value you offer to customers that they can't get elsewhere. Your UVP should be central to your customer acquisition strategy, as it's what will make potential customers choose you over your competitors.

Now that you've identified your goals, target audience, and unique value proposition (UVP), it's time to plan your tactics. These are the specific actions you will take to attract new customers. Your tactics will depend on your goals and target audience, but they could include search engine optimization (SEO), content marketing, social media marketing, email marketing, pay-per-click advertising, influencer marketing, referral programs, and more.

Your tactics should also consider the customer journey. Different tactics might be needed to raise awareness, spark interest, encourage consideration, and drive conversion. For example, SEO and content marketing can help raise awareness, while email marketing and retargeting ads can help encourage consideration and conversion.

Budget plays a crucial role in your customer acquisition strategy. You need to figure out how much you can afford to spend to acquire a new customer. Understanding your Customer Acquisition Cost (CAC) and Customer Lifetime Value (CLV) is essential here. Your CAC should ideally be lower than your CLV to ensure profitability. If it costs more to acquire a customer than they bring in over their lifetime, your business will struggle to grow. Therefore, it's crucial to allocate your budget in a way that optimizes your CAC.

Finally, it's essential to track and measure your performance. Identify the key metrics that align with your goals. These could include website traffic, conversion rate, CAC, CLV, customer retention rate, and more. By tracking these metrics, you can determine which tactics are working, which aren't, and where you can improve.

Remember, building a customer acquisition strategy isn't a one-time task. It should be a flexible plan that you regularly review and adjust based on your evolving understanding of your customers, market trends, and what works best for your business. In the next sections, we'll explore different customer acquisition tactics in more detail.

Top Customer Acquisition Techniques

Your customer acquisition techniques are the tools and strategies you use to attract new customers. Here are several proven techniques that I have already explained in the previous chapter. Just to remind you, I'm mentioning them again here:

- Search Engine Optimization (SEO)
- Pay-Per-Click (PPC) Advertising
- Content Marketing
- Email Marketing
- Social Media Marketing
- Email Marketing
- Affiliate Marketing
- Referral Programs

These techniques are not one-size-fits-all. In fact, the most successful e-commerce businesses use a mix of different techniques tailored to their goals, target audience, and budget.

It's also important to note that different techniques might be effective at different stages of the customer journey. For example, SEO and content marketing are great for building awareness, while email marketing and retargeting ads are often more effective at the conversion stage.

The next section of the chapter will delve into specific strategies and best practices for using each of these customer acquisition techniques.

The Importance of Customer Retention

For a successful e-commerce business, it's crucial to strike a balance between attracting new customers and keeping existing ones happy. Often, e-commerce players invest heavily in customer acquisition, overlooking the power of retention. However, studies show that successful customer retention can drive a business's profitability in multiple ways. Let's explore the reasons why customer retention is crucial for your e-commerce business.

1. **Cost-effectiveness:** One big reason to prioritize customer retention is cost. Studies from Bain & Company reveal that acquiring a new customer can cost six to seven times more than retaining an existing one. This statistic underlines the economic benefits of focusing on retaining customers. Strategies for retention may include efforts like customer loyalty programs, personalized marketing, superior customer service, etc. Although these require investment, their cost is often lower than the expense of customer acquisition campaigns involving SEO, PPC, and other digital advertising platforms.
2. **Increased Customer Lifetime Value (CLV):** Customer Lifetime Value refers to the total revenue a business can reasonably expect from a single customer account. Building a long-term relationship with customers can lead to higher profits, as trust grows and customers make more frequent and significant purchases. Research by Frederick Reichheld of Bain & Company suggests that increasing customer retention by just 5% can boost profits by 25% to 95%.

3. **Word-of-Mouth Marketing and Brand Advocacy:** Happy customers can be the biggest advocates for your brand. The power of word-of-mouth marketing is well-known, and in the digital age, online reviews and social media sharing have amplified its reach. An existing, satisfied customer will not only repeat purchases but will also spread positive word-of-mouth for your brand, attracting new customers in their network. This organic promotion can be more effective than paid marketing efforts.
4. **Predictable Revenue:** While new customers are often unpredictable in terms of their purchasing habits and brand loyalty, repeat customers provide predictability and stability to your revenue stream. They make purchases more regularly, and their spending patterns can be analysed more accurately. This allows for more precise forecasting and financial planning.
5. **Feedback and Improvement:** Existing customers are a great resource for feedback. They are more likely to share their experiences and give candid suggestions, which are invaluable for the continuous improvement of your products and services. These customers have seen your business evolve and are more invested in your brand. Their feedback can help you identify gaps in your offering, understand customer preferences better, and stay ahead of market trends.
6. **Advantage over Competition:** In a crowded e-commerce marketplace, having a loyal customer base gives you an edge over competitors. These customers stick with your brand despite having many options, providing you with a reliable market share. Customer retention can, therefore, be a competitive advantage.

Given these compelling reasons, customer retention should be an integral part of your business strategy. In the following sections, we will delve into effective customer retention strategies and how to implement them for a thriving e-commerce business.

Strategies for Retaining Customers

When we delve deeper into the concept of customer retention, the intricate nature of the strategies involved starts to surface. To navigate through these nuances successfully, we need to thoroughly understand various strategies that can anchor customers to your e-commerce business. However, bear in mind that these strategies are not universal laws but should be treated as guiding principles that can be moulded according to your business model, target audience, and market dynamics.

Exceptional Customer Service

Customer service is the backbone of customer retention. Businesses that understand the value of excellent customer service and go the extra mile to ensure customer satisfaction often find themselves with a loyal customer base. This strategy isn't merely about resolving customer problems; it's about anticipating issues and making the buying process as seamless as possible.

Investing in well-trained customer service personnel, employing advanced technology for efficient customer service management, and instituting customer-centric policies are some ways to improve your business's customer service.

Personalized Experiences

In today's era, personalization can act as a powerful tool in your customer retention strategy. Customers appreciate experiences tailored to their preferences and needs, which can range from product recommendations based on their previous browsing or purchasing history to personalized messages and emails.

To do this well, you often need to use fancy technology like artificial intelligence and machine learning. These advanced tools can analyse large amounts of customer data and generate insights to create highly tailored customer experiences, even in a large customer base.

Loyalty Programs

Rewarding customers for their loyalty to your brand is a proven strategy for customer retention. Loyalty programs give people a reason to keep buying from you, which can make them spend more money over time . These programs can offer various benefits - discounts, points, free merchandise, early access to new products, etc.

The key to a successful loyalty program lies in its structure - the rewards should be enticing enough to make people want to keep shopping with you, and the mechanism to earn and redeem these rewards should be simple and easy to understand.

Regular Communication and Engagement

Customer engagement is vital for retention. Regular, valuable communication keeps your brand in the customer's mind and nurtures the relationship over time. This engagement could take the form of newsletters, product updates, informative content, or personalized offers.

It's crucial, however, to strike the right balance in communication frequency to avoid spamming your customers. Every interaction with your customer should provide value and enhance their connection with your brand.

Seamless Shopping Experience

A seamless shopping experience that cuts across all customer touchpoints - website, mobile app, social media platforms, customer service - can significantly enhance customer retention. Aspects such as an intuitive, user-friendly website design, a streamlined checkout process, easy return policies, and a variety of payment options all contribute to a positive shopping experience that can keep customers coming back.

Feedback Solicitation and Implementation

Inviting feedback from customers serves two significant purposes - it makes customers feel valued and provides your business with first-hand insight into customer expectations and experiences.

Implementing these strategies is a meticulous process that demands commitment, time, and resources. However, the long-term gains in terms of customer loyalty, increased customer lifetime value, and enhanced profitability make the investment highly rewarding. As we progress further into the book, we will dissect each of these strategies, exploring their implementation in greater depth.

Tools and Resources for Customer Retention

Now that we've talked about why it's important to keep customers and discussed different ways to do it, let's look at some tools and resources that can make it easier. These tools can help you collect data, analyze customer behavior, automate communication, personalize experiences, and manage customer loyalty programs effectively. In an e-commerce environment where competition is fierce, utilizing these resources can help you maintain a strong relationship with your customers and ultimately increase your bottom line.

Customer Relationship Management (CRM) Systems

CRM systems are the technological backbone of any successful customer retention strategy. These powerful tools help businesses collect, store, and analyze customer data to manage interactions with existing and potential customers better.

Popular CRM systems like Salesforce, HubSpot, or Zoho give you a complete picture of how you interact with your customers across different points of contact . These tools help you understand their preferences, identify patterns, anticipate issues, and customize your approach to different customer segments, which is vital in retaining customers in the long run.

On top of that, CRM systems provide useful metrics that can inform your customer retention strategies and gauge their success. Metrics like purchase history, interaction history, and customer segmentation can allow you to approach customer retention in a more data-driven and targeted way.

Email Marketing Platforms

Despite the rise of various digital communication channels, email remains a powerful, personal, and cost-effective way to communicate with your customers. Email marketing platforms like MailChimp, Sendinblue, and Constant Contact make it easier for businesses to manage email communications at scale.

Not only do these platforms allow you to design and automate email campaigns, but they also provide analytics to measure open rates, click-through rates, conversions, and other key metrics. By analyzing these metrics, you can make your emails even better and keep your customers interested, which helps you keep them around for longer.

Loyalty Program Software

Managing a loyalty program can be a complex process, involving tracking customer purchases, assigning points or rewards, and handling redemptions. That's where loyalty program software like Yotpo, Annex Cloud, and Smile.io come in handy.

These tools make it easy to manage a loyalty program by doing things automatically. Plus, they help you understand how customers shop, so you can make your loyalty program even better at keeping them coming back.

Customer Feedback Tools

Feedback tools like SurveyMonkey, Qualtrics, or Hotjar play a pivotal role in gathering customer feedback. They allow you to design and distribute surveys, gather feedback in a structured manner, and analyze the data for actionable insights.

These insights can reveal areas of customer dissatisfaction, shed light on what your business is doing well, and provide suggestions for improvement. Such feedback is invaluable in refining your offerings, enhancing customer satisfaction, and improving your retention rates.

Customer Support Software

A robust customer service function is key to customer retention. Customer support software like Zendesk, Freshdesk, or Help Scout can centralize and streamline your customer service efforts.

These tools allow your customer service team to manage all customer queries, complaints, and requests from one platform, ensuring that no customer issue slips through the cracks. By integrating with your CRM system and other tools, these platforms can enable a seamless customer service experience, which is a crucial factor in customer retention.

Choosing the right tools for your business depends on your unique needs, customer base, and budget. The key is to leverage these tools in a way that complements your customer retention strategies, adds value to your customers, and supports your overall business goals. Remember, customer retention is an ongoing effort that requires continual monitoring, analysis, and optimization. In the upcoming chapters, we will further explore how these tools can be utilized effectively to 4X your e-commerce sales in 169 days.

⦸⦸⦸⦸

Every extra click, scroll, or doubt costs you a sale. Simplicity converts—every time.

CHAPTER 9

CONVERSION RATE OPTIMIZATION: TURNING VISITORS INTO BUYERS

Understanding Conversion Rate Optimization

As an e-commerce business owner or digital marketer, your main aim is to convert website visitors into customers. But how do we ensure that the individuals who land on our pages complete the purchase? The answer lies in understanding and implementing Conversion Rate Optimization (CRO).

CRO isn't just about getting someone to make a single purchase or take one step closer to buying. It's about creating an environment that makes people want to engage with your site, trust your brand, and eventually make a purchase, sign up for a newsletter, or download something like a whitepaper.

CRO involves a systematic, data-driven approach to improving your website performance, aimed at increasing the percentage of visitors who complete a desired action on your site. It requires an understanding of how users navigate your site, what actions they perform during their visit, and what obstacles prevent them from achieving your goals.

By improving your conversion rate, you're essentially maximizing the return on your existing traffic. This, in turn, magnifies the effectiveness of every other digital marketing strategy you implement. It's like squeezing more juice from the same orange.

When discussing CRO, several crucial metrics and terms need understanding:

- **Conversion Rate (CR):** This represents the percentage of website visitors who complete a specific goal. It's the number of conversions divided by the total number of visitors, multiplied by 100.
- **Bounce Rate (BR):** This shows the percentage of people who navigate away from your website after viewing only one page. A high bounce rate could indicate issues like irrelevant content, poor user experience, or slow load times.
- **Exit Rate (ER):** This denotes the percentage of visitors who leave your site from a particular page, after visiting any number of pages. High exit rates on specific pages could highlight problems with those pages that are driving users away.
- **Average Session Duration (ASD):** This metric measures the average time spent by a user in a single session. Longer durations typically indicate higher engagement levels.
- **Average Page Views Per Session (APV):** This signifies the average number of pages a visitor views during a single session. Higher page views could mean a higher level of interest or engagement.

Remember, successful CRO isn't just about improving numbers. It's about understanding user behavior, needs, and pain points and using this knowledge to create a superior user experience that encourages conversions.

CRO is both an art and a science. It combines quantitative data (such as analytics and metrics) and qualitative data (such as user surveys, feedback, and heatmaps) to create actionable insights. Based on these insights, you form hypotheses about what changes to your website could improve conversion rates.

These hypotheses are then put to the test using various methodologies such as A/B testing, multivariate testing, or user testing. The ultimate goal is to identify what works best for your unique audience. Each audience is different, and what works for one website might not necessarily work for yours. A tailored approach to CRO can not only increase conversions but also build long-term customer loyalty by delivering a superior user experience.

In the next sections, we will delve deeper into CRO strategies and how they helped achieve 4X growth in just 169 days. Stay tuned!

Conversion Rate Optimization Tools

Before diving into the specifics, it's essential to understand that the choice of a conversion rate optimization (CRO) tool can vary depending upon the size, requirements, and the strategic goals of the e-commerce business. However, certain fundamental features are necessary regardless of the business specifics, such as easy navigation, clear dashboards, and robust data analysis capabilities.

Google Analytics

Google Analytics is pretty much a must-have for any online business. It's highly versatile and free, offering a ton of useful features. With Google Analytics, you can keep an eye on things like how many people are visiting your website, what they're doing while they're there, and lots of other important metrics.

Starting with the basics, Google Analytics helps you understand who your audience is. This involves a detailed report on demographics (like age, gender, and location), the devices they use, the time they spend on the website, and even their interests.

Furthermore, Google Analytics provides invaluable insights into how the audience is interacting with the website. These behavior reports include details about the most visited pages, bounce rates, and the path users take to navigate through the site. For e-commerce, this is especially useful because it helps you find out where people might be getting stuck and not buying anything.

Optimizely

Going beyond basic analytics, Optimizely offers an opportunity to perform real-time experimentation on your website. This sophisticated tool is essentially a platform that facilitates A/B testing, enabling you to change different elements on your website to determine what leads to better conversions.

Key features include its easy-to-use interface, which lets you adjust and test various page elements without needing to write code. It also offers dynamic traffic allocation, which means that it can direct more traffic to the version of your page that is performing better.

Hotjar

Understanding how customers move through your website is key to making their experience better and getting more sales. Hotjar, a behavior analytics tool, helps visualize this journey. Its heatmapping feature offers a graphical representation of user activity on your site, showing where users click, scroll, and even where they are getting stuck.

Additionally, Hotjar provides the functionality to record user sessions. This feature allows you to replay the actual user interactions, helping you gain a deeper understanding of your user's experience. You can identify patterns and common pain points, which can be vital in forming strategies for improvement.

Crazy Egg

Crazy Egg is a tool that specializes in generating heatmaps and providing in-depth insights into how users are interacting with your website. Its distinctive features such as confetti maps and scroll maps provide a unique perspective on user behavior.

A scroll map shows you how far down the page your users are scrolling and at what point most people stop scrolling, an important insight for content placement. Overlay reports identify how many clicks each element on your webpage receives, giving you an understanding of what draws user attention.

All these tools, when used judiciously, can guide your CRO strategies, making them more data-driven and effective. As we proceed to the next chapters, we'll discuss how to attract and retain users, with the ultimate goal of converting them into loyal customers.

⦸⦸⦸⦸

Plans don't build businesses—execution does. And 169 days is more than enough if you stop waiting and start moving.

CHAPTER 10

169 Days Action Plan: Week 1 to Week 24

A Step-by-Step Guide

Welcome to the most exciting phase of this book - the 169 days action plan designed to boost your e-commerce sales by four times. This segment provides a detailed, week-by-week guide to turning your business dream into a reality. Let's embark on the journey together.

Week 1 to Week 2: Understanding your Business

The first two weeks are all about understanding your business inside and out. Assess your unique selling proposition, your areas of strength, and the facets where you might be lagging. Get to know your customers: who they are, what they need, and how you can meet those needs.. Design a comprehensive map of your existing sales funnel and pinpoint any areas where things could run smoother. Use these insights to create the basis of a robust strategy to improve your business.

Week 3 to Week 4: Building the Foundation

With the insights gained from the first two weeks, shift your focus towards the foundational aspects. Kick-start the process by optimizing your website, ensuring it is user-friendly, responsive, and easily accessible on mobile devices. Simultaneously, begin working on your Search Engine Optimization (SEO) strategy: conduct keyword research, develop a list of targeted keywords, and start implementing on-page optimization techniques.

Week 5 to Week 8: Crafting your Marketing Strategy

The subsequent four weeks should be focused on constructing and refining your marketing strategy. This includes building strategies around content marketing, email marketing, Pay-Per-Click (PPC) advertising, and social media marketing. Use what you've learned in the previous weeks to create a comprehensive marketing strategy aimed at reaching your target audience and leading them through the sales funnel.

Week 9 to Week 12: Enhancing the Customer Experience

During this phase, focus on making the customer experience on your website even better. Use the tools and insights discussed in earlier chapters to analyze user behavior and identify any areas for improvement. Use this information to remove any obstacles, simplify navigation, and ensure a smooth checkout process for your customers.

Week 13 to Week 16: Testing and Optimization

The subsequent four weeks are dedicated to testing and optimization. Implement A/B testing tools to experiment with different elements on your website and marketing campaigns. Extract insights from these tests and use them to optimize your strategies, thereby improving conversion rates.

Week 17 to Week 20: Scaling Up

Once your strategies have been optimized and are yielding positive results, it's time to scale up. Spend more money on advertising, try reaching more people, and think about trying new ways to market your stuff. You could also think about adding more things to sell or trying to sell your stuff in new places, but make sure you're still focusing on what you're really good at.

Week 21 to Week 24: Monitoring and Adjusting

In the last four weeks of this six-month plan, you need to keep watching what's happening and making changes when you need to. Watching things closely helps you see if things are getting better and catch any new problems that come up. This way, you can fix things quickly and keep your business growing.

The goal of this plan is not only to amplify your sales but also to construct a robust and sustainable business model. As you transition into the final phase of this plan, remember to stay adaptable, foster a learning mindset, and don't be afraid to make changes when necessary. Your journey towards 4X sales growth is just getting started. Keep trying new things, keep improving, and stay committed to your vision.

If you can't measure it,
you can't multiply it.

CHAPTER 11

MEASURING SUCCESS: KEY METRICS AND KPIS

Introduction to KPIs

The role of KPIs

Any venture, regardless of its nature or size, needs to keep tabs on its progress to ensure success. In the world of e-commerce, this tracking is done using Key Performance Indicators (KPIs). These aren't just numbers; they're like maps that show you where your business is going. They give you valuable information about how your business is doing, helping you make smart decisions and improve your strategies.

The Nature of KPIs

KPIs are quantifiable metrics or numbers that reflect how well a business is achieving its strategic and operational goals. For an e-commerce venture, they could cover lots of things, like how many people visit your website, what they do there, how much you sell, and if your customers are happy. What makes KPIs particularly important is their ability to turn abstract aspects like customer satisfaction and website performance into measurable, actionable insights.

KPIs in the E-commerce Landscape

In the dynamic and highly competitive world of e-commerce, KPIs serve as crucial navigational tools. They highlight strengths and identify areas of weakness in a business's operations. This insightful data can help you understand your customers better, assess your strategies' effectiveness, and inform future decisions. KPIs allow you to keep your fingers on the pulse of your business and make the necessary adjustments to keep it thriving.

Selecting Your KPIs

While there's a wide range of KPIs to choose from, it's essential to remember that not all of them may be relevant to your business. The key to effective KPI tracking is to select those that align with your business objectives and offer the most valuable insights into your operations. For instance, if your goal is to grow your customer base, metrics like website traffic, customer acquisition cost, and conversion rate might be your KPIs of choice. On the other hand, if you're focusing on customer loyalty and retention, KPIs such as customer lifetime value, retention rate, and churn rate would take precedence.

Setting Goals and Monitoring Progress

Once you've determined your key performance indicators, the next steps involve setting clear, measurable goals for each KPI and regularly monitoring your progress towards these targets. Remember, KPIs are not a one-time measurement but a continuous process of tracking and analysis. This continuous monitoring allows you to promptly identify any issues, assess the effectiveness of your strategies, and make adjustments as needed.

By effectively employing KPIs in your e-commerce operations, you not only keep track of your present performance but also get valuable insights into future growth directions. In the following sections, we will delve into some of the most crucial KPIs for e-commerce and how to leverage them effectively.

KPIs for E-commerce

1. **Traffic Metrics:** Traffic metrics serve as a pulse check of an e-commerce website. They help gauge the number of people visiting the website, the frequency of visits, the sources of traffic, and the geographical distribution of visitors.

   Total visits indicate the overall traffic on your website, including repeat visits. Unique visitors, on the other hand, are distinct individuals who have visited your site within a specific period, regardless of the number of times they visit. New sessions give you an idea of how many first-time users your site attracts.

   The source of traffic is categorized as organic, referral, direct, social, or paid. Understanding these sources can provide insights into the effectiveness of your SEO efforts, referral partnerships, social media campaigns, and paid advertisements.

   Engagement metrics then take the spotlight. These metrics show you how people are interacting with your website and content. They include average session duration (the average time spent on your site), pages per session (average number of pages viewed during a visit), bounce rate (percentage of single-page sessions), and exit rate (percentage of exits from a page).

2. **Conversion Metrics:** Conversion metrics offer insights into the percentage of visitors who perform a desired action—whether it's making a purchase, subscribing to a newsletter, or filling out a contact form. These are critical as they directly correlate to revenue and ROI.

The main conversion metric to pay attention to is the conversion rate, which tells you the percentage of visitors who actually do what you want them to do. Another important one is the average order value (AOV), which tells you how much money, on average, people spend every time they make a purchase.

Another crucial e-commerce metric is the cart abandonment rate, which shows you the percentage of people who put things in their cart but don't end up buying them. This can help you figure out if there are any problems with your checkout process.

3. **Customer Metrics:** Customer-centric metrics include customer acquisition cost (CAC), customer lifetime value (CLV), retention rate, and churn rate.

   CAC is the cost of acquiring a new customer, while CLV represents the total revenue a business can expect from a single customer account. The retention rate gives you the percentage of customers you managed to retain over a given period, and the churn rate, conversely, indicates the percentage of customers who stop doing business with you.

4. **Financial Metrics:** Financial metrics include gross revenue, net profit, average margin, return on investment (ROI), and cost per acquisition (CPA). Gross revenue refers to the total sales revenue, while net profit is what remains after all costs and expenses are subtracted from the gross revenue.

   The average margin, the difference between the selling price of a product and its cost, is crucial for understanding the profitability of individual items. ROI measures the efficiency of an investment and CPA refers to the cost of acquiring a new customer.

Understanding these KPIs will provide valuable insights into the performance and potential of your e-commerce business. In the following chapters, we'll dive into how to use these KPIs to drive growth and profitability.

Using KPIs to Drive Improvement Introduction

Utilizing Key Performance Indicators (KPIs) effectively is essential for any successful e-commerce business. It's not enough to just measure these indicators; the real power lies in how you use these metrics to drive tangible improvements in your e-commerce operations. The process involves deep analysis, setting strategic goals, implementing changes, monitoring the results, and continuously refining your strategy.

Identifying Opportunities through KPI Analysis

Your KPIs offer a wealth of insight into your business. It's through detailed analysis that you can identify opportunities for improvement. These opportunities can present themselves in various areas such as high customer churn rates, low conversion rates, low average order values, or high cart abandonment rates. Each of these areas signifies a unique challenge and an opportunity.

For example, a high churn rate could signify dissatisfaction with your product or customer service, thus, indicating an area for improvement. Similarly, a low conversion rate could imply issues with your website's usability or your marketing strategy, thereby, revealing an opportunity to refine your approach.

Setting SMART Goals

Having identified areas for improvement, you need to convert these opportunities into measurable and achievable goals. Your goals should be SMART – Specific, Measurable, Achievable, Relevant, and Time-bound. By following the SMART framework, you ensure that your goals are well-defined, realistically achievable, and can be effectively monitored over a specific period.

For example, if you're addressing a high cart abandonment rate, a corresponding SMART goal could be: "Reduce cart abandonment rate by 15% over the next quarter through checkout process optimization and an effective re-targeting campaign."

Implementing Changes – The Action Phase

Implementing changes based on your KPI analysis is the next crucial step. These changes might involve redesigning your website to enhance user experience, redefining your pricing strategy, adding new products that cater to customer preferences, enhancing customer service, or developing a new targeted marketing campaign.

The key here is to ensure that the changes are aligned with your SMART goals and implemented systematically. Also, you should establish monitoring systems to track the effectiveness of these changes.

Monitoring and Evaluating Results

Post-implementation, your focus should shift to monitoring the results. This phase involves using your KPIs to measure the effectiveness of the changes implemented and track progress towards your goals. For instance, if your goal was to reduce cart abandonment rate, closely monitor this metric to assess whether your changes are leading to the desired improvement.

The Cycle of Continuous Improvement

The process of using KPIs to drive improvement is a cyclic one, embodying the principles of continuous improvement. As soon as one goal is achieved, you should return to your KPIs, identify the next area for improvement, establish a new set of SMART goals, implement corresponding changes, and monitor the results.

By following this approach, you will foster a culture of ongoing improvement and growth within your e-commerce business, ensuring that your business is constantly adapting, evolving, and thriving in the dynamic digital marketplace. The upcoming chapter will shed light on real-world case studies, showcasing how successful e-commerce companies have harnessed their KPIs to drive impressive growth.

Problems in business don't kill growth—avoiding them does.

CHAPTER 12

Overcoming Challenges: Troubleshooting and Course Correction

Understanding Potential Pitfalls

Introduction

Embarking on an ambitious goal to quadruple your e-commerce sales in 169 days demands both a thorough plan and the flexibility to tackle potential hurdles. Businesses that effectively identify potential pitfalls ahead of time and establish protocols for addressing them stand the best chance at sustaining momentum and achieving their growth objectives. This section of the chapter provides a thorough examination of various common hurdles that may impede the expansion of your e-commerce venture, along with suggestions for avoiding or overcoming them.

Common Pitfalls

The world of e-commerce is full of challenges, even in seemingly simple areas like website design. If your website is difficult to use or takes a long time to load, customers might leave out of frustration, causing high bounce rates and fewer sales. An ineffective or improperly targeted marketing strategy could waste valuable resources without delivering the desired return on investment. If SEO is not thoroughly applied, your website may struggle to appear in the initial pages of search engine results, significantly reducing visibility and organic reach.

There are also technical challenges, like cybersecurity threats. If your website gets hacked, it could damage your reputation and cost you a lot of money. Managing inventory can be tricky too. If you don't predict demand well or keep track of your inventory efficiently, you might end up with too much or too little stock, which can hurt your profits and make customers unhappy. Relying too much on one sales channel can also be risky. If that channel suddenly stops bringing in sales, your business could suffer. And don't forget about mobile shoppers – if your website isn't mobile-friendly, you could miss out on a lot of potential customers.

Recognizing Signs of Trouble

It's crucial to catch problems early before they become big issues. If you notice a sudden drop in website visitors or fewer people making purchases, it could be a sign of trouble. Increasing complaints from customers or more people abandoning their shopping carts without buying anything are also signals that something might be wrong. Keep an eye out for a noticeable decrease in your website's ranking on search engines or clear signs that customers aren't happy with your products or services.

Conclusion: A Proactive Approach

Awareness of potential pitfalls doesn't guarantee immunity against them, but it does equip businesses with the knowledge to deal with them effectively. Proactive planning and being ready to deal with potential issues can greatly improve the resilience of your e-commerce venture. With this understanding, you'll be better positioned to plan for the worst while striving for the best, ensuring preparedness to handle any challenges that might emerge on your 169-day journey to quadruple your e-commerce sales.

In the upcoming sections, we will delve deeper into strategies for troubleshooting common e-commerce issues, provide guidance for effective course correction, and share inspiring real-world examples of businesses that have weathered significant challenges to achieve extraordinary e-commerce growth.

Strategies for Overcoming Challenges

Reframing Challenges as Opportunities

In the world of e-commerce, encountering challenges is inevitable, but how you approach and resolve these issues will shape the course of your business. It's essential to view challenges not as impassable barriers, but as chances for growth, innovation, and improvement. Embracing this mindset is the first step in effectively addressing potential hurdles.

Technical Challenges and Solutions

Technical issues, from website crashes to cybersecurity threats, can have significant implications for your e-commerce business. Ensuring a seamless user experience is paramount, which calls for constant website maintenance, rigorous performance testing, and swift troubleshooting. As such, having a reliable IT team or outsourcing these tasks to a trusted partner is an investment that can pay dividends in the long run.

In addition, investing in cybersecurity cannot be overlooked. Given the sensitive nature of data that e-commerce platforms handle, robust measures such as SSL certificates, two-factor authentication, and data encryption should be implemented. Conducting regular security audits will help identify potential vulnerabilities, while having a detailed emergency response plan will ensure prompt action in the event of a security breach.

Addressing Strategic Missteps

Strategic challenges often emerge from ineffective marketing efforts, subpar SEO outcomes, or underperforming customer acquisition and retention strategies. In such scenarios, it's essential to employ data-driven tactics to identify issues and adjust strategies.

For instance, if a marketing campaign isn't performing well, analyzing A/B testing results or user engagement metrics can provide valuable insights. Similarly, if SEO efforts aren't yielding the desired outcomes, conducting an SEO audit can help pinpoint weak keywords or issues with website optimization. When facing challenges with customer acquisition or retention, delving into customer feedback and reassessing your value proposition can offer actionable solutions.

Overcoming Operational Hurdles

Operational challenges can encompass various issues, such as inventory mismanagement, logistics inefficiencies, or supply chain disruptions. Leveraging technology is often a solution in these instances. Inventory management software, for example, can provide real-time insights into inventory levels, enabling accurate demand forecasting and efficient restocking. In the event of supply chain issues, having a diversified supplier network can provide alternatives and keep your operations running smoothly.

Building Resilience through a Growth Mindset

Finally, instilling a growth mindset within your organization is vital. A growth mindset sees challenges as opportunities for learning, encouraging resilience and continuous improvement. Remember, the journey to quadrupling your e-commerce sales in 169 days will not be without hurdles. However, with each issue addressed, your business grows stronger, paving the way to your ultimate goal.

When and How to Pivot

Recognizing the Need to Pivot

In the e-commerce industry, a business must be flexible and responsive to the ever-evolving market dynamics, changes in consumer behavior, advancements in technology, and internal operations. Knowing when to pivot or shift strategy can mean the difference between success and failure.

A pivot is not always an indicator of a failing business strategy. It can often be a demonstration of an enterprise's adaptability to changing circumstances. A crucial element of recognizing the need to pivot is to monitor trends, performance metrics, customer feedback, and competitive movements consistently.

Understanding the pain points of your business and evaluating your strengths can provide valuable insights into the need for a pivot. Observing the performance of different products or services and their profitability can reveal if certain aspects need more focus or if they need to be phased out.

Types of Pivots

- **Customer Needs Pivot:** If you discover that your product or service addresses a different problem or fulfills a more urgent requirement than originally assumed, a pivot based on customer needs might be required. The shift could be subtle or significant, depending on the discrepancy between the initial and newly identified customer need.
- **Platform Pivot:** This involves transforming a single product or service into a platform that can host multiple complementary products or services, or vice-versa.
- **Business Architecture Pivot:** It involves a shift from a high margin, low volume business to a low margin, high volume business model or vice-versa. This decision would typically be influenced by market trends, competition, and consumer purchasing power.
- **Value Capture Pivot:** This involves changes to your approach for generating revenue, such as altering the pricing model, introducing tiered offerings, or adopting a freemium model.
- **Technology Pivot:** If a company can deliver the same customer value through a superior, more efficient technology, it might decide to pivot. This could involve adopting emerging technologies like AI, blockchain, or machine learning.
- **Channel Pivot:** This is a change in sales or distribution channels. A company might decide to switch from retail to e-commerce, or from a direct sales model to a partnership model, and so on.

Making the Decision to Pivot

It's essential that the decision to pivot is data-driven. Collecting and analyzing customer feedback, tracking performance metrics, surveying market trends, and studying competitors can provide critical insights that indicate the need for a pivot. A combination of quantitative data (like sales figures, website traffic, conversion rates) and qualitative data (like customer testimonials, reviews, survey responses) can provide a holistic understanding and strongly signal the necessity to change direction.

Executing the Pivot

Upon deciding to pivot, businesses need to craft a comprehensive plan to transition smoothly. This includes defining new objectives, outlining actionable steps, and identifying necessary resources. It's also necessary to set realistic timelines and create a roadmap that clearly delineates responsibilities and milestones.

Transparent communication is vital in this process. Ensure that all stakeholders, including employees, customers, partners, and investors, understand why the pivot is necessary and how it will benefit them. Detail the new strategy and how it aligns with the company's long-term vision. A well-managed pivot can re-energize a company, opening up new avenues of growth and profitability.

Growth isn't found in comfort zones. It's earned in the uncomfortable decisions.

CHAPTER 13

CASE STUDIES: SUCCESS STORIES AND LEARNINGS

Introduction to Case Studies

Why Case Studies?

As we approach the final chapter of our journey, it's important to recognize that while theories are crucial, they alone cannot fully predict real-world outcomes. To truly understand the mechanics of e-commerce success, we must explore practical, real-life examples of businesses that have thrived in the industry. This is where case studies prove their value.

Case studies provide an in-depth understanding of how concepts work in real-life scenarios. They offer a comprehensive view of how businesses face challenges, apply strategies, and achieve their goals. By analyzing success stories and learning from their experiences, readers can gain valuable insights and apply these lessons to their business endeavors.

Scope of Case Studies

In this chapter, we'll look at various case studies from the Indian e-commerce landscape. Each case study will be an exploration of how a particular e-commerce business has harnessed the principles, strategies, and tools discussed in the previous chapters.

We will break down their success into measurable components, align them with the strategies we have discussed, and evaluate their effectiveness. This process will allow us to learn not only from their successes but also from their mistakes and setbacks.

The case studies will cover a range of businesses—large and small, established and startups, catering to various sectors. The objective is to provide a diverse spectrum of experiences and insights to accommodate the varied needs and contexts of our readers. The hope is that these real-life stories will not only inspire but also guide and motivate you to achieve your e-commerce aspirations.

Get ready to explore fascinating stories of successful e-commerce businesses with us. We'll uncover valuable lessons and insights as we journey through these engaging narratives.

Flipkart - Mastering the Indian E-commerce Market

The Inception and Early Days

Sachin Bansal and Binny Bansal, both alumni of the prestigious Indian Institute of Technology (IIT) Delhi, started Flipkart in 2007. Inspired by the success of Amazon, they left their jobs at Amazon to bring the same model to India. Initially, Flipkart was a modest online bookstore operating out of an apartment in Bangalore.

However, what set them apart was their vision to transform the e-commerce industry in India and their focus on customer service from the very start. For example, when they started, they personally delivered books to customers to understand their needs and feedback better. They were committed to making sure the customers were satisfied with their purchases.

Expanding Horizons - Venturing into New Categories

By 2010, Flipkart began selling CDs, DVDs, mobile phones, and mobile accessories. They understood the pulse of the market and realised that the demand for electronics, especially mobile phones, was on a steep rise. They made strategic alliances with mobile phone brands to launch exclusive models on their platform.

One such tie-up was with Motorola in 2014 for the exclusive launch of Moto G in India. This move revolutionized the mobile phone market in India and set a new standard for exclusive smartphone launches. It was a win-win situation for both the parties - the phone brands could penetrate the Indian market without needing a physical store, and Flipkart could attract a massive user base.

Pioneering Customer-centric Initiatives and Innovations

Flipkart has been a trailblazer in many aspects of e-commerce. Recognizing the discomfort Indian customers had towards online payment, they introduced 'Cash on Delivery (CoD)', which was unheard of at that time. This helped to instil trust among customers, and soon, other players in the market followed suit.

Understanding the complex Indian landscape, they built their own logistics network, Ekart, to ensure smooth delivery. They pioneered the easy return and refund policies which have now become a standard in the industry. Their 24x7 customer service was another initiative that resonated with customers.

Strategic Acquisitions and Future Prospects

Over the years, Flipkart made several strategic acquisitions. They acquired the fashion e-commerce platform Myntra in

2014. This move helped Flipkart establish a strong foothold in the online fashion industry in India. Later, they acquired Jabong, thereby further strengthening their position in the fashion segment.

In 2018, the US retail giant Walmart bought a majority stake in Flipkart. This bolstered Flipkart's financial muscle and paved the way for future growth.

The Flipkart case is a powerful demonstration of how customer-centricity, deep understanding of the market, strategic planning, and innovation can take an e-commerce startup to incredible heights. The lessons from Flipkart's journey can provide valuable insights for anyone looking to venture into the e-commerce sector.

Case Study 2: Nykaa - Redefining Beauty and Personal Care E-commerce in India

The Beginning and Vision

Nykaa is an Indian retail seller of beauty, wellness, and fashion products, founded by Falguni Nayar in 2012. After a successful career as an investment banker and managing director at Kotak Mahindra Capital Company, Falguni started Nykaa with a vision to create an inclusive space for Indian women, providing them access to a comprehensive selection of curated beauty products.

Initially operating as an online retailer, Nykaa's business model revolved around delivering a seamless online shopping experience with a wide range of products, detailed product information, and expert advice on beauty trends.

Establishing Brand Trust and Loyalty

Nykaa aimed to provide consumers with an unparalleled selection of authentic and quality products. The company committed itself to a no-fake policy, ensuring that all products sold on the platform were 100% genuine. This helped establish trust among customers, which is particularly essential in the beauty and wellness industry.

To boost customer engagement, Nykaa launched an online Beauty Book Blog and a series of YouTube tutorials featuring industry experts and influencers. They introduced the 'Nykaa Network' - a beauty advice forum where users can discuss beauty-related topics, ask questions, and share advice.

Omni-channel Retail and Product Expansion

After solidifying its online presence, Nykaa ventured into offline retail, opening its first physical store at T3 Terminal, Indira Gandhi International Airport, New Delhi, in 2015. It adopted an Omni-channel retail strategy to create an integrated and cohesive customer experience no matter how or where a customer reaches out.

Recognizing the immense potential in the Indian beauty market, Nykaa began introducing its own line of beauty products in 2015, starting with nail enamels. Today, Nykaa's in-house collection spans across cosmetics, skincare, personal care, and fashion.

Future Prospects and Growth

In recent years, Nykaa has ventured into men's grooming and fashion, further expanding its market reach. The brand has also been able to attract investment from key global institutional investors, boosting its growth trajectory.

The journey of Nykaa serves as a powerful case study of how an understanding of consumer needs, authenticity, customer engagement, and an Omni-channel strategy can lead to success in the e-commerce industry. This story also shows us the great opportunities in niche e-commerce markets and the importance of curating customer experiences.

BONUS CHAPTERS AHEAD!

You've already explored 13 chapters full of ideas to grow your e-commerce sales. But I felt there's still more value I can give you—so I added two bonus chapters with fresh insights that you won't want to miss.

And that's not all...

Q-Commerce is the Next Big Thing.

We're already working on a dedicated sequel that will focus only on Q-Commerce—platforms like Blinkit, Zepto, and Instamart, how to get started, what mistakes to avoid, and how to grow your brand faster in this 10-minute delivery world.

So go ahead, read the bonus chapters now.

And stay connected, because the next book is coming soon with even deeper strategies to help you win big.

CHAPTER 14

UNLOCKING EXPORT OPPORTUNITIES VIA E-COMMERCE: THE AMAZON.COM ADVANTAGE

Introduction

As global e-commerce continues to surge, Indian sellers are presented with an unprecedented opportunity: exporting to international markets through global online platforms. Among them, Amazon.com (USA) has emerged as a powerful gateway for Indian products to reach millions of international customers without the need for traditional export channels.

From bedsheets made in Panipat to natural supplements from the Himalayas, Indian products are gaining immense traction globally. With low entry barriers and rising international demand for quality, affordable goods, the time for Indian sellers to export via e-commerce is now.

Why E-Commerce Export Works

Traditional exports involve high investment, complex logistics, and multiple layers of intermediaries. E-commerce, however, eliminates many of these frictions. Here's why it works:

- Direct Access to Global Consumers
- No Need for Physical Stores or Agents
- Easy Brand Building through Reviews & Ratings
- Scalable Logistics via Amazon FBA (Fulfilled by Amazon)
- Regulatory Simplicity with India's Export Incentives for E-Com

Key Steps to Start Selling on Amazon.com from India

- Register as an Amazon Global Seller
- Select Products with Global Appeal
- Ensure Compliance (IEC, GST, AD Code)
- Use FBA for Warehousing and Fulfilment
- List Products with Optimized SEO Titles and Images
- Run Ads (PPC) to Drive Initial Traction
- Collect Reviews and Build Social Proof

Winning Sectors for Indian Exporters on Amazon.com

India's traditional strengths in textiles, Ayurveda, personal care, and home decor are being rediscovered by U.S. and global buyers online.

Low cost + high quality + rich heritage = a winning formula.

Real Stories – Indian Sellers Going Global

- A Jaipur-based bedsheet brand saw a 4x sales increase in 6 months selling fitted sheets and towel sets on Amazon USA.

- An Uttarakhand herbal brand exported Shilajit and mineral supplements using FBA, reaching 50 states in 90 days.
- A Mumbai-based jeweler went from local store sales to international demand for spiritual rings and incense within 3 months of listing.

Future Outlook

With rising global trust in Indian manufacturing and Amazon opening more cross-border opportunities, we expect the next 5 years to see a 10x increase in Indian e-commerce exporters. Government schemes like ONDC export integration and simplified customs clearance further strengthen the case.

The question is no longer if you should start exporting through e-commerce, but how fast you can get started.

Annexure: Top Performing Indian Products on Amazon.com (U.S. Market)

1. Sheet & Pillowcase Sets
2. Scrub Bottoms
3. Eau de Parfum
4. Scrub Tops
5. Area Rugs
6. Toothbrush Replacement Heads
7. Towel Sets
8. Eau de Toilette
9. Fitted Sheets
10. Mouthwash
11. Rings
12. Pillowcases
13. Incense

14. Trace Minerals
15. Dish Cloths & Dish Towels
16. Toothpaste
17. Decorative Urns
18. Shilajit
19. Cloth Napkins
20. Blended Vitamin & Mineral Supplements

Closing Thought

Indian sellers are no longer restricted to domestic markets. With the right product, process, and platform, you can transform your small business into a global brand. E-commerce is your bridge, Amazon is your highway, and Nextgen is your navigator.

Let the world be your customer.

Success doesn't come from knowing more; it comes from doing more with what you know.

CHAPTER 15

Quick Commerce (Q-Commerce): Winning in the 10-Minute Economy

Introduction to Q-Commerce

The world of e-commerce is no longer just about convenience. It's about instant gratification. Enter Quick Commerce (Q-Commerce) – the evolution of online retail that delivers essentials and daily-use products in as little as 10 to 30 minutes.

From busy professionals to young digital natives, today's consumers expect products to reach them almost as quickly as they decide to buy them. This isn't a trend; it's a consumer revolution.

The Rise of the 10-Minute Economy

Urbanization, changing consumption habits, and the growth of hyperlocal logistics infrastructure have given rise to what we now call the 10-minute economy. Whether it's fresh groceries, medicines, or last-minute personal care items, Q-Commerce is designed to fulfill high-frequency, low-ticket-size orders rapidly.

What's driving it?

- ➢ Hyperlocal dark stores
- ➢ Rider fleets optimized through technology
- ➢ Millennial impatience and Gen-Z expectations
- ➢ The 'buy-now, get-now' mindset

Q-Commerce vs. Traditional E-Commerce

Parameter	Traditional E-Com	Quick Commerce
Delivery Timeline	1–3 days	10–30 minutes
Product Focus	All categories	FMCG, daily needs
Order Size	Larger cart	Small & frequent
Fulfillment Model	Central warehouse	Hyperlocal stores
Platform Examples	Amazon, Flipkart	Blinkit, Zepto, Instamart

Business Models in Q-Commerce

Q-Commerce isn't one-size-fits-all. Here's how platforms are structured:

- ➢ **Inventory-led (e.g., Blinkit, Zepto):** The platform owns inventory in dark stores.
- ➢ **Marketplace Hybrid (e.g., Swiggy Instamart):** Mix of inventory and local seller fulfillment.
- ➢ **Aggregator Model (e.g., Dunzo):** Ties up with multiple sellers and delivers on demand.

Each model impacts seller onboarding, inventory management, and pricing.

Challenges of Q-Commerce

While the speed is impressive, the model comes with its own hurdles:

- **Operational Burn:** High logistics cost per delivery
- **SKU Planning:** Limited shelf space needs high-velocity products
- **Rider Dependency:** Workforce reliability is crucial
- **Profitability Pressure:** High CAC (Customer Acquisition Cost), low margins

Despite the challenges, Q-Commerce is seeing massive investor interest due to high repeat rates and brand stickiness.

Opportunities for E-Com Sellers

E-commerce sellers can tap into Q-Commerce by:

- Listing fast-moving SKUs on platforms like Blinkit & Zepto
- Using Q-Commerce for sampling, new product launches, and building brand recall
- Expanding regional brands into metro markets with hyperlocal fulfillment

Q-Commerce enables brands to stay top-of-mind and top-of-feed.

Onboarding to Q-Commerce Platforms

To join this ecosystem, sellers typically require:

- GST Registration and FSSAI License (for consumables)
- Product samples & packaging aligned with Q-Commerce standards
- Regional APOBs or VPOBs to ensure GST compliance in fulfillment zones

Nextgen Business Support Services Pvt. Ltd. plays a critical role here, assisting sellers with:

- APOB & VPOB registration
- Fulfillment partner coordination
- Documentation, compliance & onboarding support

Role of Virtual Offices & APOB

Q-Commerce demands local presence for GST and logistics eligibility. Here's where Virtual Places of Business (VPOB) and Additional Places of Business (APOB) become game changers. They allow sellers to register across multiple zones without investing in physical warehouses.

Nextgen helps simplify this expansion with:

- Ready VPOB locations
- APOB compliance
- Coordination with logistics partners

Marketing & Growth Tactics

Growth in Q-Commerce is built on micro-moments. Brands can win with:

- App-based advertising (Blinkit Ads, Zepto AdTech)
- Geo-targeted SMS & WhatsApp campaigns
- Flash discounts & in-app banners
- Leveraging delivery experience to earn repeat buyers

Customer experience is key. **Speed + product quality = loyalty.**

Case Studies & The Road Ahead

Case Study: Regional FMCG Brand Expansion via Blinkit

A homegrown brand expanded into Delhi, Kolkata, and Mumbai in 60 days using Nextgen's VPOB & APOB services.

Results:

- 2.5x increase in daily orders
- 30% of customers reordered within 15 days

What's Next?

- Voice-enabled orders
- Drone delivery pilots
- Expansion into Tier 2 cities

Closing Thought

Q-Commerce is redefining immediacy in retail. It's not a substitute for traditional e-commerce but a high-frequency complement. For brands willing to adapt, it presents a rare opportunity: the ability to be not just fast, but first.

In a world of speed, Q-Commerce is your competitive edge.

PARTNER WITH NEXTGEN ON YOUR E-COMMERCE JOURNEY

Thank you for reading _"*4X Your E-Commerce Sales in 169 Days*"!

I hope this book has empowered you with knowledge, inspired you with success stories, and supported you in turning your e-commerce dreams into profitable realities.

Whether you're a first-time seller or a growing brand ready to scale across India and beyond, **Nextgen Business Support Services Pvt. Ltd.** is your end-to-end partner in navigating the world of:

- **E-Commerce Growth**: Platform onboarding, cataloging, marketing, performance tracking
- **Q-Commerce Acceleration**: Blinkit, Zepto, Instamart onboarding, APOB/VPOB, ready-to-sell services
- **Global Expansion via Exports**: Amazon Global Seller, compliance, warehousing, payouts & banking
- **Compliance Made Easy**: GST, FSSAI, trade licenses, PTAX, and more
- **Virtual Office Services PAN India**: VPOB in most major states to support GST compliance and multi-state fulfilment

- **APOB Services**: Hassle-free Additional Place of Business registration to meet local logistics and legal requirements

With 10+ years of domain experience and tech-enabled infrastructure, we help you sell faster, smarter, and stronger — across borders.

Reach Out to Us

Email: support@nbsspl.com, rajevrk@nbsspl.com

Website: www.nbsspl.com

Call: +91 89812 22369 | **WhatsApp:** +91 91470 70619

Head Office: Kolkata, West Bengal | PAN India Operations

Let's co-create your success story.

With Best Wishes,

CA Rajev Harlalka

Nextgen – Your Partner in Progress.